Sketches

Of

His

Presence

Count your blessings

J. David Scherling

Sketches

Of

His

Presence

God's Powerful Influence in My Life

J. David Scherling

Dedication

[17]O God, you have helped me from my earliest childhood—
and I have constantly testified to others of the wonderful
things you do. [18]And now that I am old and gray, don't
forsake me. Give me time to tell this new generation (and
their children too) about all your mighty miracles.
Psalm 71:17, 18 (Living Bible)

To my grandchildren

Amelia Anne

Anna Maria

Benjamin David (already with the Lord)

Elizabeth Candace

Hannah Carissa

Isaiah Daniel

John Daniel

Josiah Luke

Kassandra Lynn

Samantha Pearl

Table of Contents

Preface – Introduction

Sketches of His Presence—Introduction

Before my dad, William Howard Scherling, died in 1975, he encouraged me to write a book about my life story. He was proud of me, his only son, and he could see God at work in my life and thought it would be good for me to share with others some of those incidents. Although I considered the possibility and even began to tape record some of the stories of my early life, the thought of writing my autobiography was a little overwhelming.

My cousin, Dr. Steven Scherling, a university professor and business consultant, in May of 2006 asked me if I had written my book. Quoting Ros Singleton, "There is a book within every one of you," he added that we all should make an effort to share our story. I lamely replied that I had written books (study guides that were never published) and had published articles (technical engineering papers) but did not feel adequate to write a book.

It was Steve Saint's book, *Walking His Trail, Signs of God Along the Way,* that twisted my arm as he urged all his readers to write down for their children and grandchildren the wondrous ways that God has shown Himself faithful. Stories of God's presence, leading, and provision need to be shared for His glory, as well as to inform those who love us. Writing one story at a time did not seem quite as overwhelming as a whole autobiography and I felt like it was something I could do. God is good, and it is my prayer that these sketches of His presence will encourage you to write your own stories also.

These "sketches" are arranged by category and therefore are not necessarily in chronological order. Even though some are interrelated, please consider each as an individual story of God's special provision. In instances where I have not succeeded in obtaining permission, names of people, places, and groups have been changed and I apologize for these discrepancies.

Acknowledgments

[16] I have never stopped thanking God for you. I pray for you constantly, [17] asking God, the glorious Father of our Lord Jesus Christ, to give you spiritual wisdom and understanding, so that you might grow in your knowledge of God. [18] I pray that your hearts will be flooded with light so that you can understand the wonderful future he has promised to those he called. I want you to realize what a rich and glorious inheritance he has given to his people.[19] I pray that you will begin to understand the incredible greatness of his power for us who believe him. Romans 1:16-19 (New Living Bible)

While studying at Oak Hills I took these verses as my "life's verses" and have prayed this prayer of the Apostle Paul for myself and for my family. I now pray this prayer for all those who graciously gave inspiration and guidance for the writing of this book.

First, I want to thank my children—daughter Valerie and her husband, Ed; son Bill and his wife, Toni; and son Steven and his wife, Catie—for their love, honor, encouragement, and direction for these *Sketches*. God has blessed me with wonderful children. He is helping them raise my grandchildren so that their parenting far outshines my own.

I also want to thank those who read the manuscript and commented with such insight—Rod Broding, Raschelle Johnston, Claudia LaValleur, and artists Stephen Henning and Sue Roche, both of whom also offered help on the illustrations. Special thanks to my son Steven who provided untold computer graphics expertise.

Most of all, I want to thank my lovely and talented wife, Delores, who read and reread the manuscript multiple times and each time made excellent constructive suggestions. She researched *The Chicago Manual of Style 15th Edition* until she could quote it for her recommendations. More significantly, I thank her for her love, dedication, and support, without which I could not have lived my life filled with dramatic illustrations of God's powerful influence.

John D. Scherling   John C. Goodrich   William H. Scherling

1 – What a Heritage!

Be very careful never to forget what you have seen God doing for you. May His miracles have a deep and permanent effect upon your lives! Tell your children and grandchildren about the glorious miracles He did. Deuteronomy 4:9 (Living Bible)

My mother, Eleanor Pearl Goodrich Scherling, was born into a family of six children in 1911 and grew up in Pillager, Minnesota. Her siblings were, in order of birth, Cora, Earl, Edith, Eleanor (my mother), John, and Lillian. Although they professed to be nominal Christians, she told me that when she was quite young they were not very spiritually minded and did not attend church often.

One day, in 1919 or 1920, when the four older children were in school, my grandmother, Etta Goodrich, was not feeling well and decided to go to the doctor, who lived and practiced in Motley, about ten miles west of Pillager. In those days a train ran from Brainerd, east of Pillager, to Staples, west of Motley, in the morning and returned in the afternoon. Grandma bundled up John and Lillian and caught the morning train to Motley, saw the doctor, and returned home in the afternoon. On the way back, the train stopped halfway between Motley and Pillager and picked up a farmer who had "flagged" the train. As he made his way down the aisle of the passenger car, his eyes fell on five-year-old John, and as he walked past little Johnny, the farmer placed his hand on John's head and said, "This young man is for God."

John never forgot those words. When he was older, he went to the little church there in Pillager and found the Lord as his Savior. Together with his older sisters, he evangelized the whole family, including my mother. She also began to attend the little Baptist church, and as she grew up, fell in love with that train-flagging farmer's youngest son, Billy, and married him—my father.

John went on to become a pastor, church planter, and missionary to the native peoples of northern Canada. As a "bush-pilot"-evangelist, he reached many small native communities that were not approached by others. He founded Continental Mission and served as director of the mission for many years. He then was invited to serve as pastor to missionaries in Brazil, the Philippine Islands, and other parts of the world. He also founded Worldwide Ministries and served as director of this mission for several years. At 93, he still ministers to many people who love and appreciate him.

My dad, William H. Scherling, studied formally only until the eighth grade. He learned the photography business from his brother Arvid, who was not only a successful businessman, but also an evangelist and international speaker and author. Dad bought his own photo studio in Bemidji, Minnesota, in 1937 and operated it until a year before he died in 1975. He was self-taught in theology and taught adult Sunday school and was a lay preacher for many years. He initiated the first Christian radio program broadcast from the Bemidji radio station KBUN. It was a weekly 15-minute broadcast of recorded hymns and devotional comment by him. He would record the program from his office on tape and bring it to the station every week until other Christian programs began to be aired.

One day when I was a graduate student at Trinity Evangelical Divinity School, Deerfield, Illinois, Dad came to visit. I asked him if he wanted to attend class with me and he readily accepted the invitation. I don't remember the subject of the theology class that day, but I do remember that it was very technical and beyond my comprehension. After class I apologized to Dad for bringing him to such a difficult class. On the way home he explained the whole thing to me—he understood and was familiar with the subject.

Not only was Dad a student of the Word, but also a man of prayer. Although I have never had malaria, while we were in Brasília with Wycliffe Bible Translators, generally a non-malaria area of Brazil, I came down with a fever that seemed to me to be something similar. One minute I was shivering with the cold and could not get warm even covered with

Malaria—Tropical Killer
Malaria is a tropical disease spread by mosquitoes and characterized by severe chills and fever. In the early 1900's, many workers died from malaria while building the Panama Canal, railroads, and other civil projects in the tropics. While we were in Brazil, several of our colleagues, working in the jungle, suffered severely from malaria and were, at times, near death from it. While we were in Indonesia, 1999 to 2001, two missionaries on the Island of Papua died of malaria. It is a very real threat to people working in the tropics.

many heavy blankets. The next minute I was sweating

profusely and not able to get comfortable in bed. This went on for a couple of days, during which time I was not able to get up, eat, or sleep. Then early one morning the fever left and I got up, ate, and went to work.

Later that day my dad called on the phone, which was an unusual occurrence, because he was from the old school when long distance phone calls were a luxury, and where we were living, on the Wycliffe campus in Brasília, there was only one phone at that time. When someone from the outside called, the person who answered the phone had to run all over campus to find the person the phone call was for. When Dad finally got me, he asked if I was all right. I said, "Sure, why?" He explained, "Last night God got me out of bed in the middle of the night to pray for you. Why would He do that?" When we checked the times, allowing for the time zone difference, it was the exact time the fever left me.

Knowing you have family—biologically and/or spiritually—praying for you is very important and reassuring. When our daughter Valerie was three and a half years old, and our son Billy was one month old, we left home for Wycliffe

Bible Translator's Jungle Camp training in southern Mexico. After six weeks at "Main Base" where we studied, worked, and experienced jungle training as a group, it was time for us to go out in the jungle to a place, relatively secluded, to learn to live there on our own. It was a two-day hike, over the mountains on muddy trails, in the rain; at noon on the second day we arrived at the place we would call home for the next six weeks.

It was still raining as I hung the "jungle hammock"—a hammock with a roof on it—and laid sleeping Billy in his basket to continue his nap while Delores prepared lunch. I finally found enough dry wood to start a small fire and boiled some water from our canteens in a pot for soup. When it was ready, we sat down on a muddy wet log to eat our soup and tostados—toasted tortillas—and peanut butter. As was our custom, little Valerie prayed first. As she prayed, my heart was overcome with emotion—what was I doing here? There I was, a graduate civil engineer, a Naval officer—a "can do" Seabee type—a candidate for a master's degree in Biblical Studies, and I was at the end of my rope, afraid I could not go on. Valerie said, "Daddy, it's your turn." I was all choked up and could not pray. The thought had just occurred to me—if I could just phone home, my dad and church family would pray and God would provide the strength I needed to continue. When God nudges you to pray for those serving Him on the mission field or wherever, do it. They are depending on your prayers. We survived—people **were** praying—God is good!

———————

Delores's family also has a rich heritage. Her dad, Vernon Fultz, was a strong leader in his home, in church, where he served on the Trustee Board, in a young boys' ministry called Sky Pilots, where he was one of the "Commanders," and on the Camp Shamineau Board. Delores was greatly influenced musically by her dad's mother, who played the piano in church and helped pay for Delores's piano lessons.

The family of Delores's mother, Roberta, also grew up in church, and knew and loved the Lord. Although Grandpa Blase (her mother's father) was not wealthy, he had a sensitive heart and obeyed the Lord. One time when we came home from Brazil in the winter and we did not have extra money for winter clothes, Grandpa Blase came to me and said, "Do you need a new coat?" And placed enough money in my hand to buy a new winter coat.

My Heart's Desire

2 – My Heart's Desire

Delight yourself in the Lord and He will give you the desires of your heart. Psalm 37:4 (New International Version)

One day during family devotions, when I was four, my mother asked if I wanted to invite Jesus to come into my heart. I responded, "Yes," and prayed to receive the Lord as my Savior. This did not make me a perfect boy, by any means, and although I was not a real bad boy, I could have been much better. I especially enjoyed sports and played them all, but was not an outstanding athlete. My favorite was basketball, and although I made the junior high teams (as last man), I was cut in my sophomore year. I continued to play, of course, in intramurals and church league. When I was fifteen my dad helped me get my first car and a part-time job during high school helped me keep it running. I was very proud of the cars I owned during those teenage years. I also enjoyed the girls and did not have much trouble getting the attention from them I enjoyed so much. As you can see, the things I loved—basketball, cars, and girls, as well as other things, kept me occupied and there was little time for the Lord.

But God wanted me to "delight myself in Him." Mom and Dad were on the Board of Continental Mission during those years, and every month board members and other supporters would meet at our home to pray, on their knees, for the missionaries in northern Canada. I would often participate and could feel the Lord's leading me to serve Him as a missionary. On occasion I would admit that "I may have to be a missionary some day." (Webster defines "missionary" as "a person sent on a mission, esp. on a religious mission." For these sketches, I would clarify "sent by God, and funded by His people, individually or corporately.")

During the spring of my senior year in high school, 1955, my church held a series of special meetings. They were called "Deeper Life Meetings," and the speaker shared that as Christians we could live in close communion with God. As I attended those meetings, the Holy Spirit convicted me that I was not living a life consistent with how He would have me live. So when the speaker invited us to come forward and ask God to help us live the deeper life, I responded. As I knelt at the altar I prayed, "Lord, I know I am not living as I should. I want a closer walk with you." His response was immediate, "Dave, your problem is that you think too much of your car.

If you sell your car, you and I can be just like this." And He held up one hand with two fingers tight together. I said, "Lord, that car is me. I can't do that. I'll still be a Christian, won't I?" He confirmed to me that, yes, I would still be a Christian. I got up and went back to my seat in the last row.

After high school I started college, but dropped out after two quarters. I moved around from job to job and found myself in south Texas working as a draftsman for the City of Harlingen. In February of 1958 my buddy Mark and I got homesick, quit our jobs, and went back to Bemidji. While I stayed with my folks for a couple of weeks my mother gave me the books *Through Gates of Splendor* and *Jungle Pilot* to read. The Holy Spirit began again to speak to my heart.

In those days there was a recession in the U.S. and people said there were bread lines in the Twin Cities. However, I decided that down there, in the Twin Cities, would be the best place for me to try to get a job. I went to downtown Minneapolis at 8:00 a.m. on a Monday morning and was working for a consulting engineer by 10:00 a.m. (I knew I was not that good. Was God trying to get my attention?)

I found a room to rent a few doors from where my sister and brother-in-law were living in south Minneapolis, and they invited me to eat suppers with them. They were attending Salem Free Church, not far from their home, so I would go to church with them. After a couple of weeks Don, my brother-in-law, announced that there was going to be a special youth dinner at church the next Saturday evening and asked if I wanted to go with them. I said, "No, I don't think so." So Don responded, "Well, if you don't go what will you eat, because we're going?" That made me change my mind as I enjoyed eating.

The special speaker, a pastor, was preaching during the weekend on "Finding God's will for your life." That night, after dinner, he spoke on "God has a plan for your life." I was a draftsman and my job was to draw plans. A plan was something someone followed to build something by. I thought about my life. During the last three years I had dropped out of college and worked at six different places. It did not look like I was following a plan. The next morning I went to church as usual. The pastor again spoke on "God has a plan for your life." Since I could tell the Holy Spirit was speaking to me, I decided to make a decision. It was this: if the pastor speaks on the same subject at the evening service, then I would make a decision.

Well, you guessed it. He spoke on "God has a plan for your life," and although the church was full, he was speaking just to me because when he gave the invitation I was the only one to respond. As I knelt at the altar I prayed, "God, I want to know your plan for my life." Again His response was immediate. "Do you remember three years ago when you said 'no'?" I had not thought about that in three years but conceded, "Lord, you can have the car." (I had just smashed it up.) He said "I don't want the car; I want you." Since I did not know what that meant, we negotiated for a while there at the altar. God wanted me to go to Oak Hills Christian Training School and I wanted to be an engineer. He seemed satisfied and gave me peace when I consented to go to Oak Hills and seek His will for my life while studying there.

Since I had six months before school started in the fall, I went back to my old life of having fun. I had no idea what was ahead for me. The single guys at Salem Free Church were nice guys, all had good jobs, and I enjoyed doing many things with them that summer. However, just guys together can get old and so some of them started to spend more time with the girls at church. My friend Ed and I decided that we needed to look elsewhere and I remembered that I knew some nice girls at Brooklyn Center Free Church. So one Sunday night we decided to go there and look. The girls were nice, not overly warm, but did invite us to stay for the youth "singspiration" to be held there after the service. While waiting for young people from other churches to arrive, we went out to the foyer and there was a group of girls near the front door. My friend introduced us and we found out that they were from Crystal Free Church. One of the girls was named Delores Fultz. I already knew a Fultz family from Bagley, who seemed exceptionally nice and very talented, so I decided it might be worthwhile to get to know Delores. I was especially pleased when she said she would be at the college-age retreat at Buffalo Camp the next weekend and we could see each other there.

At the retreat I found out that she was not directly related to the Fultz family I already knew but I could see she was lovely with dark curly hair, was witty and fun-loving, loved the Lord, and wanted to be a missionary. I had found the "Love of my Life." What I found out later was that she was the president of the youth group and played the organ at Crystal Free Church. That same weekend, three years later, we were married. God blessed me beyond my wildest expectations, and I have had occasion to admit, when people have come up to me and complimented me on my lovely and talented wife, that I married "way over my head."

Then while I was a student at Oak Hills, God not only showed me very clearly that He wanted me to serve Him as an engineer on the mission field, but allowed me to be a "starter" on the Oak Hills basketball team as well. I also sang in the choir, and when another car was needed for the spring concert tour, my dad helped me get my first brand new car. God had given me the desires of my heart. What a blessing!

As our family grew, I found that God continued to fulfill the desires of my heart, though in ways I could not have imagined. When we went to Brazil to serve with Wycliffe Bible Translators eight years after our wedding, it never occurred to me to consider what my father-in-law was feeling when I took his firstborn daughter and his only grandchildren to the other side of the hemisphere. I thought that it was the answer to his prayers. But when a zealous and dedicated missionary took **my** firstborn daughter and **my** only grandchild to the other side of the world, Indonesia, half of my heart went with them. Even though I had prayed from before Valerie was born, that God would find the man of His choice to be her husband, and that she would find His very best for her life, when she left for Indonesia, my heart hurt. Yes, it was an answer to my prayer, but I really missed them.

When Valerie called and told me the location of their assignment in the jungle, I was devastated. She had previously told us that there were three options for them. Two were in established locations with airstrips and one was in an unestablished area, without an airstrip and a two-day walk—

through a leech-infested jungle—to the nearest airstrip. I had seriously and persistently prayed that the Lord would send them to a place where they could be reached easily and where communication with the outside was good. I suspected, however, before she told me, where they were going—to the unestablished location. She could tell I was in tears when she told me of the assignment. She clarified, "But, Dad, a church in Oakland, California, has taken on this group as their 'Adopted People Group' and they have already sent out teams to build a house for the missionaries whom God is sending there. We believe we are those missionaries."

God is good and generally there have been helicopters available to transport them and visitors to the village of Obukain. However, one time she did have to walk the two-day trek out to the nearest airstrip when she was pregnant with Isaiah. It took twelve years for the people of the village to finish their own airstrip. Today there is a good airstrip and Valerie and her family live in a house made from solid hardwood, no longer in one made from insect-infested tree bark. She also has a satellite phone and I can call her at any time. She uses it to inform us of prayer requests and family updates.

———

The old Gene Pitney country song goes *"Only love can break your heart; only love can mend it again."* Much has been written attempting to explain the incredible power of love. I learned a lot about love when Valerie was born. The love I felt for her was something that I had never felt before. The love that I had for my mother was different than the love I had for my wife, but the love I felt for my firstborn was new and very unlike the others. When she was very young, still an infant, she became sick with a high fever. We worked "feverishly" to get her temperature down, but to no avail. Finally we took her to the emergency room at the hospital. The doctor said she needed a shot of antibiotic to fight the infection that was causing the fever. I never liked to take shots and always resisted taking them, but this time I wanted to take that shot for her. What kind of love was this? Can you imagine what love it took for God to give His Son to die for us?

Valerie went on to graduate at the top of her class at the American School of Brasília. Then at Oak Hills Christian College and Trinity International University she earned every scholarship available and was honored as top student at Trinity by the governor of Illinois. She taught one year at a Christian school in Florida and then God called her to serve on the mission field. She met Ed at missionary training and they have four children, Hannah, Elizabeth, Isaiah, and Josiah.

All of my children have honored me with their love and their lives. Good-looking and athletic, our oldest son, Bill, was and is everything a father wants in a son. He played on the conference champion soccer team in high school. Unfortunately, I did not get to catch many of his games that year because we had moved to Chicago for my work and Bill chose to stay in Minnesota for his senior year of high school. I struggled with feeling like a poor father, missing Bill and the opportunity to cheer on his championship team. When he played for Pillsbury College and went to the National Christian College Athletic Association National Championship tournament in Georgia, we went to all the games. What wonderful memories I have of cheering on the third place Pillsbury team!

Bill graduated from Mankato State University in automotive engineering. His senior class project was to design and build a "kit" car. The body design was primarily his responsibility. The class finished the project and completed the prototype on time and within budget. I was so proud of his work that I requested another body from the same mold, as well as a running chassis from the project jigs. Although the car remains part of my car collection in storage, it is licensed and ready to go.

Bill went to school with an ROTC scholarship and serves in the Army Reserve. He served in Bosnia in 2002 as Commander of a small peacekeeping base and at this writing, has orders to Afghanistan for 2008, where he serves as the leader of a small Army engineering team.

Generally I pray that God would provide opportunities for my children and grandchildren to serve Him wherever they are. Bill spent his first 15 years in Brazil and is bilingual. Once when he was sent to Honduras with the Army, he had a chance to visit a local church with one of his fellow reservists who happened to be a pastor. The pastor was asked to speak but did not know Spanish, and no one in the congregation could interpret for him, so he spoke in English and Bill translated into Spanish (with a Portuguese accent).

Bill married his high school sweetheart, Toni, and together they have three lovely daughters, Kassie, Sami, and Anna Maria. I was really honored when, in 2006, I toured the new Guthrie Theatre in downtown Minneapolis, where Bill was on the project management team putting on the finishing touches. The Guthrie is awe-inspiring—incorporating designs never before done in a building.

Our youngest son, Steven, continues the tradition of honoring his father in all he does. He plays tennis and was my best friend while we lived in Tallahassee. He graduated from North Florida Christian High School at the top of his class and attended university with a full scholarship from the

State of Florida. At the University of Florida, Steven began to take leadership in InterVarsity Christian Fellowship and appreciated the opportunity to have spiritual influence in the lives of several students. On occasion, when he

> **_USS Maine SSBN 741_**
> The *USS Maine* is a 560-foot-long nuclear powered submarine armed with 24 intercontinental ballistic missiles, affectionately called a "Boomer". Maine class submarines patrol the coasts of the U.S. but can only fire their missiles by presidential command. They rarely need refueling, but return to home port for food and crew changes.

would bring them home with him, they would thank us, with tears, for Steven. After graduating in civil engineering, he served in the Navy as a nuclear power engineer aboard a submarine. One of the highlights of my life was when he invited me out to sea on the *USS Maine* for a weekend.

After fulfilling his commitment with the Navy, Steven transferred to the U.S. Public Health Service as an environmental engineer. He is currently assigned to the Indian Health Service in Bemidji, Minnesota.

Steven was introduced to his future wife, Catie, when she was his cousin's roommate at Wycliffe's linguistic training at the University of North Dakota. She displayed all of his desires in a wife (even including her middle name, Anne). Together they have a daughter, Amelia Anne, and a son, John Daniel.

I love my children and grandchildren. How precious it is to know the love of family, especially at times when your heart feels like it is breaking. My prayer is that the love of our family will be so evident that their hearts will be mended, when needed, and that they will learn, as I did, that if they "delight themselves in the Lord," "He will give them the desires of their hearts."

"C" Clip

3 – Prayer Changes Things

The earnest prayer of a righteous man has great power and wonderful results. James 5:16 (Living Bible)

When we served in Brasília, we enjoyed worshipping with the English-language fellowship called the Union Church, which met in the Lutheran Church building on the south side of town. It was a rare occasion when I was asked to speak because others in the congregation were excellent speakers and the pastor seldom took a

> ### *Brasília—Capital of Hope*
> In the 1950s President Juscelino Kubitscheck, in an effort to open the interior of Brazil, moved the national capital from Rio de Janeiro, on the coast, to a central, undeveloped area of the high plateau and named it Brasília. The city was designed in the shape of an airplane. The fuselage holds the government buildings as well as the cultural centers and sports arenas. In the north and south wings, are residential and commercial areas, including schools and churches. The plan worked—the interior of Brazil is now blooming and productive.

Sunday off. I was invited once in a while, however, and when that happened I wanted to hear what the Lord would have me share with this group which included missionaries, diplomats from the international community, and some Brazilians who enjoyed speaking English.

On one such occasion I really should not have accepted the invitation because I was too busy to do justice to a sermon. On the Friday before the Sunday I was to speak, I had not prepared and was quite nervous about the assignment. While I was in my office praying (and worrying) about what I was going to share, I remembered a book I had at home that I wanted to review to help me make the decision. Our apartment was just a few hundred feet away on the Wycliffe campus, so I walked home to get it.

On the way back I met Mabel, a Baptist missionary and professor at the Baptist Seminary, who was living on our campus. She was carrying a small portable tape recorder. "Am I glad to see you!" she exclaimed as I approached. "Can you help me? This tape recorder is my roommate's prize possession and it has eaten up my tape." I didn't need this—another delay to keep me from working on the sermon for Sunday. But what could I do? It was an American tape recorder and it was often difficult to find someone to fix these things in Brasília. I conceded, "Let me look at it."

I took it back to my office and removed the cover from the drive mechanism. I could see that the tape was wound around the spindle that keeps the tape speed constant and that the little rubber roller on the spindle was held on by a "C" clip that was about 1/8th inch in diameter. If I lost that "C" clip, I would be in big trouble because it was highly unlikely that I would find a replacement part in Brasília. So, I carried the tape recorder down to the electronics shop to work on the bench there. (The Wycliffe missionary who was the electronics technician was off on assignment elsewhere, so I was stuck with the problem myself.) I tried extra hard to be very careful and contain the clip as I attempted to remove it to get at the tape wound around the spindle. But, sure enough, the clip sprang off and utterly disappeared! I immediately started to look for the clip, but it was nowhere to be found. I searched the top of the work bench and then swept the floor on my hands and knees. Then I repeated the process. As you can imagine, I was getting more and more frustrated by the minute. Further delay—and I was in no mood to joyfully be the Lord's servant!

Finally, about an hour later, Mabel found me there in the shop. She asked cheerfully, "How is it going?" I managed to say that I had good news and bad news. The good news was that the tape was unwound and in good shape; the bad news was that I had lost the "C" clip that held the roller on the spindle, could not find it, and the tape recorder was useless without it. I told her that I had been looking for it for an hour and it was nowhere to be found. "Have you prayed about it?" She asked matter-of-factly. I confessed, "No, go ahead." I was so frustrated; there was no way I could pray. But I closed my eyes and prayed with her. When we opened our eyes, there on the bench beside the tape recorder was a small piece of paper, about two inches by two inches. In the middle of that piece of paper was the "C" clip! God had answered her prayer, and mine—I now had the subject for my sermon on Sunday.

When I was in college, the InterVarsity Christian Fellowship leadership encouraged us to meet with fellow students for prayer and Bible study. I found that I really needed this, not only for the benefits of prayer and spending time in God's Word, but because of the accountability it provided. I needed help staying consistent spiritually. Meeting with a small group for prayer and Bible study became part of my life and something I have enjoyed everywhere God has led me.

In Brasília we met for breakfast and prayer in a local hotel. A typical breakfast in Brazil consists of very sweet hot milk with a little very strong coffee, and maybe, a small loaf of French bread with cheese and jam. Most restaurants were not open for breakfast, but there were many small coffee shops that served coffee and bread. In an effort to be more European, hotels often served a continental breakfast with fruit, danishes, scrambled eggs, and ham. We would go through the buffet line and then find a corner table where we could eat breakfast while we shared our concerns and prayed for each other. Among those who met with me in those days were the headmaster of the American School, the high school principal, an Army General serving as the U.S. Military Attaché, and Emmit Young, a Presbyterian missionary and chaplain of the Brazilian National Congress.

Part of Emmit's ministry was to encourage spiritual activity among the leaders of the nation. In this effort he led a small group of Brazilian senators and representatives to the Presidential Prayer Breakfast in Washington, DC. They were so enthused with this program that they inaugurated a similar program in Brazil and planned a Presidential Prayer Luncheon for interested government and religious leaders. A couple of weeks prior to the first Presidential Prayer Luncheon, Emmit came to our prayer breakfast and requested prayer for himself, as he was going that morning to meet with the president's chief of staff to ask him to choose which Scripture the president would read at the luncheon.

At that time the government of Brazil was a benevolent military dictatorship. The people elected the members of congress, but the president was selected from top military officers to serve for a maximum of five years. Emmit had a heart for the people, and had selected two Scriptures for the chief of staff to choose from. One was John 14— *"Let not your heart be troubled..."*—a beautiful and meaningful, well-known and loved portion of Scripture. The other was Isaiah 58. The prophet here is condemning the nation of Israel because they were superficially worshiping and not living as God would have them live. Some of the pertinent verses are:

58 "Shout with the voice of a trumpet blast. Tell my people Israel of their sins! ² Yet they act so pious! They come to the Temple every day and seem delighted to hear my laws. You would almost think this was a righteous nation that would never abandon its God. They love to make a show of coming to me and asking me to take action on their behalf. ³ 'We have fasted before you!' they say. 'Why aren't you impressed? We have done much penance, and you don't even notice it!'

"I will tell you why! It's because you are living for yourselves even while you are fasting. You keep

right on oppressing your workers. [4] What good is fasting when you keep on fighting and quarreling? This kind of fasting will never get you anywhere with me. [5] You humble yourselves by going through the motions of penance, bowing your heads like a blade of grass in the wind. You dress in sackcloth and cover yourselves with ashes. Is this what you call fasting? Do you really think this will please the LORD?

[6] "No, the kind of fasting I want calls you to free those who are wrongly imprisoned and to stop oppressing those who work for you. Treat them fairly and give them what they earn. [7] I want you to share your food with the hungry and to welcome poor wanderers into your homes. Give clothes to those who need them, and do not hide from relatives who need your help.

[8] "If you do these things, your salvation will come like the dawn. Yes, your healing will come quickly. Your godliness will lead you forward, and the glory of the LORD will protect you from behind. [9] Then when

you call, the LORD will answer. 'Yes, I am here,' he will quickly reply. Stop oppressing the helpless and stop making false accusations and spreading vicious rumors! [10] Feed the hungry and help those in trouble. Then your light will shine out from the darkness, and the darkness around you will be as bright as day. [11] The LORD will guide you continually, watering your life when you are dry and keeping you healthy, too. You will be like a well-watered garden, like an ever-flowing spring." Isaiah 58: 1-11 (New Living Bible)

Emmit asked us to pray that the chief of staff would choose Isaiah 58. And we did as he asked. I really believed and expected that the chief of staff would choose Isaiah 58 for the president to read at the luncheon. Later that afternoon I called Emmit and asked how the meeting went. "He chose John 14," Emmit lamented. I responded that notwithstanding our preference for Isaiah 58, John 14 was a wonderful portion and God would use it for His glory.

On the day of the first Presidential Prayer Luncheon in Brazil, President João Figueiredo, on national television, got up to read the Scripture. He said, "I've been asked to read John 14, but I'm going to read Isaiah 58." And he did, but just a few of us knew exactly why. God had answered our prayer in a way we could not have imagined! You may remember that President Figueiredo was the last military president. The next president was elected by the people.

———

Sometimes God answers the prayers of His people in ways that dramatically involve us; we may not know they are praying or the details of why they are praying until later. This next "sketch" is one of those times. As a private pilot in Brazil, I took every opportunity to fly that I could possibly afford to take. Not only did I enjoy flying, but I needed the time behind the wheel to keep my license current and keep my flying skills proficient. My friend Al Reasoner, a Presbyterian missionary, was senior pastor of twenty or thirty very small churches scattered around the remote areas north of Brasília. He called them "Preaching Points" and on Sundays when he could not be there, lay preachers held services for the congregations. With long distances and difficult, unimproved roads between them, he often flew to his churches in a small Cessna 182, landing on rough, primitive airstrips.

When he had room in the plane, and I was available, he would ask me to go with him for a weekend or for the day. On these occasions, he would let me fly left seat and he would act as instructor-pilot. I enjoyed not only the flying, but also the opportunity to fellowship with my friend and to minister to people in very remote areas.

One day we were flying north of Brasília to a location where he would be preaching that evening. Al was pointing out the various places where he would sometimes stop when he said, "Over there, to the right, is São José. Hey, I need to stop there. Head in that direction and I will show you the strip." It's a good thing he was there because I don't think I could have found it—just a trail heading up the mountainside. We landed and taxied to the top of the strip and turned the plane around. As I got out of the plane, four men rode up on horseback and talked excitedly to the pastor. They said that the day after Al had been there, two weeks previously, one of the young men of the village broke his leg (playing soccer) and was not able to get to the hospital. The hospital was in a town about ten miles away, but there were no roads, only trails, and he was hurt too badly to ride a horse. Would Al take him to the town and the hospital? Of course we would. I will never forget the scene—the men carrying their buddy to the plane. His leg was green and the broken bone was sticking out. We put him and his pretty wife in the back seat of the plane and took off. We radioed the town and asked for the ambulance to meet us at the airport. We turned the patient and his wife over to the doctor and left for our next appointment.

About a year later I went again with Al, this time to hold services at São José. We landed, taxied to the top, and turned the plane around. I got out and soon four guys rode up on horseback. This time, however, one of them was the fellow who had suffered the broken leg. I greeted him, "Hey, I remember you. Last time I was here you had a broken leg." He broke into a big grin and said, "It was a miracle! If you had not stopped that day, I would have died." Those were his words—the whole village had been praying and God brought us there in answer to their prayers.

Sometimes our prayers are answered differently than we expect. In 1975 my dad was dying of cancer. In June of that year I was representing the Brazil Branch of Wycliffe Bible Translators at their biennial business conference in Mexico City. My sisters and I decided that we would fast every Wednesday noon, wherever we were, and spend that time praying for our dad's healing.

This particular Wednesday while I was in Mexico City, I sat down in my room and began to pray. As I prayed for dad's healing, I decided to go through Mark's Gospel and claim the promises the Lord Jesus made for us here on earth.

I came to verse 24 of Chapter 11. Jesus is talking to His disciples:

> *[24] Listen to me! You can pray for anything, and if you believe, you will have it. [25] But when you are praying, first forgive anyone you are holding a grudge against, so that your Father in heaven will forgive your sins, too." Mark 11:24, 25 (New Living Bible)*

I wanted to claim verse 24, but then I read the condition in verse 25. I did not think I had a grudge against anyone, so I prayed verse 25 in a general way. Then God reminded me, "What about so-and-so (He named the person) that bugged you during Summer Institute of Linguistics training? You need to ask his forgiveness for your attitude." I had not seen this individual since linguistic training several years before. I got up from my prayer table, went to the cafeteria where the conference attendees were eating lunch, found him, and asked his forgiveness. He had no idea that there was a problem and forgave me.

I went back to my room and began again to claim verse 24 for my dad's healing and verse 25 in general. God said again, "What about so-and-so (God mentioned another person by name also) that bugged you during Jungle Camp Training?" Again, I had not seen this person since Jungle Camp and the conference was the first time we had been together since then. So once again, I got up from the table where I was praying and went to the cafeteria, found him, and asked his forgiveness for my unChristlike attitude. He also had no idea what I was referring to but readily forgave me.

My dad went to be with the Lord in a few months, but I was healed.

Prayer changes things!

Building 1—Brasília

4 – Construction

Unless the LORD builds a house, the work of the builders is useless. Psalm 127:1 (Living Bible)

During my year at Oak Hills, God clearly impressed on me that he wanted me to serve Him as an engineer on the mission field. So the next year I returned to Bemidji State College and the following year transferred to North Dakota State University, where I graduated in 1963. In the meantime the Selective Service officers did not think I was a serious student and wanted to draft me out of college, so to continue toward my goal of becoming an engineer, I joined the Navy Reserve to keep from being drafted.

To tell the truth, I rather expected God to get me out of my obligation with the Navy Reserve, and had actually applied and was accepted at a seminary in Minneapolis. But God had other plans. After graduation I worked for a consultant for six months and then began my career in the Navy. I'll never forget the day I left for Naval Officer Candidate School (OCS), November 22, 1963, because President Kennedy was shot while I was on the plane to New York City. After completing OCS and Naval Civil Engineer Corps Officers School, I was assigned to the Public Works Office at the Naval Station in New Orleans. Experience gained while working for the City of Harlingen, the Beltrami County Highway Department, and various consultants, had prepared me for the design and construction of streets, roads, bridges, drainage, water supply, and sewage disposal. Then, in addition, at the Naval Station in New Orleans, I gained administrative experience in building construction, as I was responsible for several large apartment and office building projects.

God was reminding me of the work He had for me. In New Orleans we attended a church that emphasized missions and His purpose was often before me. In fact, during this time I wrote to ten different mission agencies asking if they needed a civil engineer. I heard back from less than half of them and most of those missions which responded said, "No. Why don't you get a seminary education?" So after my four years in the Navy I enrolled at Trinity Evangelical Divinity School in Deerfield, Illinois.

The first mission agency to visit campus that year was Wycliffe Bible Translators (WBT). I had not written to them because I thought they needed only Bible translators. When

I sat down at lunch time across from the visiting missionary, Wycliffe author Hugh Steven, I asked if Wycliffe needed any civil engineers. He reached into his pocket and pulled out a long list and read, "Yes, we need two, one in Ecuador and one in Papua New Guinea." I reluctantly said, "Send me the paper work." And that started our relationship with WBT. I was secretly hoping for a nice small mission that I could easily relate to and here I was, joining one of the largest mission organizations ever. Didn't God know my limitations?

It would take another year to get to a field because we needed to complete Wycliffe's training, Summer Institute of Linguistics and Jungle Camp, as well as finish my degree at Trinity. When the subject of our field assignment came up, both of the needs from the previous year had been filled with other engineers and now the urgent need for a civil engineer was in Brazil. As we were assigned to Brazil, again I was apprehensive, because Brazil was one of Wycliffe's largest fields with five centers throughout the country. Was I biting off more than I could chew? I would definitely need His help.

In November of 1969 we arrived in Belém, Brazil, near the mouth of the Amazon River, and waited for our shipment of barrels to arrive by boat. The month spent at Wycliffe's Belém Center was good orientation to the climate and the friendly ways of Brazilians, as well as an introduction to Wycliffe-Brazil. Stopping in Brasília on the way, the next month was spent at the Cuiabá Center, where I did a survey of the property and made some suggestions for a master plan of the campus.

Finally, after Christmas we were sent back to Brasília and moved to a small Brasília suburb, Planaltina, for language study. Our administrator's apparent uncertainty of what to do with their new civil engineer did not bother

WBT-Brazil

Wycliffe Bible Translators had been invited to Brazil in the 50s and set up offices in small, crowded spaces in Rio de Janeiro. In the 60s when the government moved to the new capital in Brasília, Wycliffe also moved their leadership and rented small, cramped office and living accommodations. For over ten years the missionaries had been asking God to provide a place for them to live and work more efficiently.

me at the time. However, while in Planaltina we learned that Wycliffe-Brazil had requested a civil engineer to design and supervise the construction of the WBT-Brazil headquarters complex, but did not have the funds to start the project.

Brasília was a planned city, the new national capital, and new construction needed to follow a rigorous code, which even the officials were unsure of. Just before we arrived, the Federal District officials had found an area in the city where a mission headquarters could be constructed—after rejecting two other proposals by Wycliffe-Brazil. Still, there were no funds for construction.

It was while we were in Planaltina that the Apollo 13 mission took place. We were learning Portuguese and had met some of our neighbors, but could not yet hold in-depth conversations. The day that the Apollo 13 mission experienced their re-entry crisis, Seu Bichinho, our neighbor across the street and proud owner of the only television set for blocks around, came over and pled with us to come and watch the re-entry of the mission. I had seen several moon trips on TV and was not overly excited about this one, but he finally convinced me that there was a problem and I needed to see it. When I entered his small living room, there were about ten other neighbors, all sitting around the TV on straight-backed chairs. The astronauts had just regained contact with Houston and as I looked at the faces of the neighbors I could see that they were all crying—tears streaming down their faces. I learned that day that the U.S. space program was not just ours, but the space program of the whole free world and God had just answered their prayers.

Sometimes God blesses us with people who will become lifelong friends. We experienced this very special blessing in Planaltina. A university student, Edmundo, from Planaltina, found out that there was an American family renting the small house at the entrance to the town—a place he passed every day, going to and from the university. At first he stopped by to practice his English, but then he stopped by just to visit, almost every day. After we moved back to Brasília, he continued to keep in touch and does so to this very day.

We stayed in Planaltina for only three months. God had supplied the money for the construction of the first building,

67

so we cut our Portuguese study short and went to work. A special friend of Wycliffe founder "Uncle Cam" Townsend had sent Wycliffe–Brazil $100,000. Just to put that into perspective, the first building was 36 feet by 210 feet, three stories high and constructed of reinforced concrete. The total cost was about $5.00 per square foot. The building contained twelve apartments of varying sizes, some office space and a "group house" (a small motel-type portion of the building that housed visiting missionaries and guests).

About the time we finished the first building, an agency of the German government gave us $150,000 for the administration building. This building housed not only the administrative offices, but also a library, large comfortable study cubicles, a spacious meeting room, and a state-of-the-art publications facility. After the second building was finished, the mission "sold" individual apartments, at subsidized rates, to the missionaries living in them and thus we were able to raise the funds for the third and last building. God had answered the prayers of His servants!

With a crew of about forty workers, a construction superintendent, and foremen for the various specialties, the engineer/construction manager (me) continually felt a little overwhelmed. As spring was coming I decided to write to my old InterVarsity staff friend back at North Dakota State University, and ask if there was an engineering student who would like to come and help me during the summer. He presented the need. Terry and his friend Lenny, both North Dakota farm boys and engineering students, responded. They were a lot of fun and a tremendous help to me. Terry came back after he graduated and took over for me, finishing the third building and the gym at the American School. Then, to top it all off, he married my secretary! In the meantime, I asked for more help and was sent Bob Presler. Bob and Stella and their family are from Minnesota and fit right in with our group. Bob, a tool and die maker, grew up on a North Dakota farm and could do anything.

The soil around Brasília is red clay. When a load, like a building, is placed on clay and rain falls on it and some of the rain water is absorbed into the clay, the clay particles tend to line up and compact, causing the building to shift and settle. Therefore, the buildings in Brasília required pilings often as deep as 60 feet to get down to a firm gravel foundation. Clay is also a problem when it comes to landscaping. It is super hard and difficult to dig or smooth out with a rake. When it came time to finish the surface around the new buildings, I began to pray for a bulldozer to help move and smooth out the clay lumps.

About that time I went to Belém for another reason and happened to mention to an American helper living on the Belém campus about the need we had in Brasília for a bulldozer. He said, "I have one on a farm about 100 miles north of Brasília that you can have if you go get it." It seemed too good to be true, but when I got back to Brasília and mentioned this to Bob, he said he could get it going, so let's go get it. We set a date and a colleague who had a crew cab pickup drove us to the farm. On the way Bob stopped at a drug store to buy a bottle of ether. It took a while, but we finally found the dozer a long way off the road. After we hooked up a battery, Bob poured some ether into the air cleaner and amazingly, the big diesel roared to life. The bulldozer had been sitting idle for over a year, and when we moved it, we found a nest of snakes under it. Bob went back a week or two later and picked up the bulldozer with a big truck. The dozer needed a hydraulic pump to work the blade—I found one in Rio and Bob adapted it. We used the refurbished bulldozer to finish the landscaping on the whole campus and then sent it to our center in Porto Velho for use there.

One Saturday afternoon an incident occurred that has often reassured me in matters of truth-telling. After the construction crews working on the third building had left for the day, I was drawn to the miniature soccer field we had set up for the kids on our campus. Our sons had invited their friends from the neighborhood to come and play soccer.

During a break in the action, one of the neighbor boys came over to me and asked, "Are you the coach?" (I may have been yelling too much.) "No," I replied, "I am Billy's dad." (They all knew who Billy was.) About that same time I looked up and saw two official-looking gentlemen walking toward me on the sidewalk. As I stood up and approached them, one asked, "Are you the owner of this project?" "No," I replied, "I am the engineer." This was a lesson to me in telling the truth. In a matter of minutes, two individuals had asked me questions about who I was, and I told the truth each time, but gave completely different answers.

———

God had shown Himself powerfully faithful in some major facets of construction of the Brasília Wycliffe head-quarters—government approval granted, funds timely received, expert helpers sent. He also proved Himself faithful in the minor things that meant so much to me at that time, such as innovative construction techniques.

Innovations incorporated into the buildings included Styrofoam forms that stayed inside the concrete floors and served as sound insulation between the floors. These forms suddenly appeared on the market just as I was researching lighter-weight alternatives to the hollow clay tiles generally used in this type of construction.

Brazil was the leader in the design and production of fiber-cement roof tile panels, and about the time we started on our project two of the major fiber-cement companies developed a deeply undulated roof tile that spanned twenty feet, just the length needed for the project.

The first building featured a balcony that wrapped around the entire top floor and served as an outdoor corridor. This balcony required a handrail to keep people from falling off. I designed one that could be made efficiently and installed by the crew we employed, however the project would require a welding machine and an experienced welding technician. The equipment was not hard to find, but we would have to train the welder and I had no idea how to do it. Amazingly, one of our sharp, young laborers taught himself and manu-factured all of the railings. God is faithful!

While my primary task was to supervise construction in Brasília, I was blessed to be able to help in other areas also. About that time the Wycliffe pilots in Cuiabá, about 500 miles west of Brasília, asked me to design a hangar for the airplanes used in their area. I noticed that hangar-like build-ings in Brasília were arch-type structures with the arches made of reinforcing rod welded together. The first phase of the Cuiabá hangar was to be 60 feet wide and 30 feet long. The arch had to span 60 feet. I drew out a parabolic curve on the floor of one of the buildings and designed a section that the welding tech could produce. He welded together three arches and also the twenty-two built-up steel purlins that would run horizontally between the arches. A 60-foot arch is too long to load onto a truck, so we cut them into three pieces and sent them to Cuiabá. I went over there after they arrived and welded the arches back together and assembled them in place.

The pilots in Belém (at the mouth of the Amazon River, about 1200 miles north of Brasília) also asked me to design a hangar for their aircraft. The hangar for Belém was built using their own technician, but with a regular truss-type structure. The roofs for the Amazon Valley Academy in Belém and the American School of Brasília gymnasiums were designed similarly to the hangar at Cuiabá. For construction in the Amazon jungle area, I designed some hangars using timber trusses. One was a floating hangar, built on huge logs that formed a raft that served as the floor of the hangar. God was using me in ways I could never have imagined!

About the time the Brasília headquarters construction was being completed and we had been in Brazil for almost four years, it came time for us to go back to the U.S. for a while to bring our supporters up to date on our work. I was concerned about what I would share with our supporting churches and friends. True, God had miraculously provided funds and personnel for the headquarters project, but what had I done to further the real purpose of Wycliffe's presence in Brazil, translating the Bible for those groups who did not have the Scriptures in their own language? One day as I was taking pictures to prepare my ministry presentation, I walked into one of the translator's offices and found Dr. Loraine Bridgeman working there. "Bridge," as we called her, was from Minnesota and we enjoyed a common area heritage. I shared with her my consternation about not really feeling a part of the main purpose for Wycliffe's being there, Bible translation. On the two large tables where she was working, she had spread out the concordance, a computer printout of the words in Kaiwá language, with examples of how they are used.

She declared, "You tell your people this: this is the first time I have had the chance to lay out this concordance and use it as it was meant to be used. If you had not been here to build this building I would still not be able to use it. Furthermore, this morning I was translating in Jonah and I came to the part where he was on the ship and the storm was about to sink the ship. The crew "cast lots" to find out why

the ship was in peril and the lots fell on Jonah. They asked him about it and he told them he was running away from God. The words that concerned me were the words the crew said to him then: 'Why did you do that? You know what we have to do now.' As I looked up what I thought were the

> ### *Making a Concordance*
> A concordance is initiated by the translator recording native language speakers' conversations and stories and then transcribing the texts into a computer. The computer lists each word in alphabetical order with the phrase in which it appears in each context. The translator can then look up a word in the printout and see how that word was used in order to confirm its appropriateness for the context of the passage being translated.

right words to use, in the concordance, I found the exact same words, in context, that I needed."

Bridge explained by reminding me that when our family had visited her in the Kaiwá village, I wanted to be of help, so she gave me a small one-burner gas stove to work on. As I was trying to fix it, it really broke and there was no fixing it, so I went to town and bought her a new one. When Bridge asked her translation helper to describe how she happened to get a new stove, the helper said in her own Kaiwá language, "When he broke the old one, his wife said, 'Why did you do that? You know what we have to do now.'" "See," Bridge emphasized, "you are involved in Bible translation!"

Three New Airplanes in Brazil

5 – Mission Aviation

²Send us around the world with the news of your saving power and your eternal plan for all mankind. ³How everyone throughout the earth will praise the Lord! Psalm 67:2, 3 (Living Bible)

Often the only viable means of transportation in the remote areas of the world is the airplane. Stories of God's provision for His work and workers through aviation are abundant. The Wycliffe Bible Translators (WBT) policy, upon entering a country, is to contract with the government through their sister organization, the Summer Institute of Linguistics (SIL), to study the native languages of the country. In Brazil, the SIL contract was with a major university. Aircraft brought into Brazil to transport missionaries to the tribal villages and back were given to the university in accordance with the contract. Naturally there were risks along with the benefits with this kind of donation. The aircraft benefited both the university and SIL for several years, and many at the university saw God's love through those donations. There came a point, however, when the university wanted to use the airplanes for other purposes. This meant that SIL was not able to use the planes in the same ways as before for their work with the indigenous people groups.

While we were constructing the first building in Brasília, I noticed some worn-out aircraft at the airport and on the beach at the lake. When I asked about them, I was told that they were the ones God had provided for WBT to use under the university contract, and that unfortunately they had been allowed to fall into disrepair. Shortly thereafter, the university offered these two aircraft for sale. WBT bought them back, fixed them up, and sent them to another country for service. During our Wednesday evangelistic time for the construction workers, I used these aircraft as an example of God's love for us—God made us and loves to guide us. We often make mistakes that allow our lives to fall into disrepair and become less useable in His hands. Graciously, however, God sent His Son to die for us and purchase our redemption, fix us up and send us to the fields, "white unto harvest."

In the early 70s when the WBT Brasília Headquarters project was nearing completion, the Wycliffe administration in Brazil was asking the Jungle Aviation and Radio Service (JAARS), the Wycliffe aviation group, for additional aircraft.

They were told that it takes a lot of work to raise the funds for one airplane, let alone the three that Brazil was requesting. If Brazil would assign someone to help at the aviation headquarters, that person could be a big help in raising the funds and getting the planes to the field. So the Brazil director asked me to go to JAARS, in Waxhaw, North Carolina, for a few months of the time we would be in the U.S. visiting our supporting churches.

Shortly after we moved to North Carolina, the JAARS director encouraged me by mentioning that there was a group in Atlanta who had begun to raise the funds for an aircraft. The project had stalled and no real effort had been made to raise funds for a year or two and the aircraft to be provided had not yet been assigned to a specific mission field. If the group in Atlanta were willing to assign the plane to Brazil maybe that would be the encouragement they would need to finish raising the required funds. I went to Atlanta to meet with the group. It was helpful that Uncle Cameron Townsend, founder of Wycliffe Bible Translators, went with me, because that was all the encouragement the group needed and soon all the funds were in for the first airplane, a Cessna 206.

About that time a homebuilder from Maine went to Brazil to build a house in a tribal village for a WBT missionary. When he returned to Maine he was so enthusiastic that he wanted to raise funds in Maine for another airplane. He was a pilot himself and flew an amphibian aircraft that was built in Maine, the Lake Buccaneer. He wanted to get a Lake Buccaneer for the work in the Porto Velho area of Brazil where many of the villages served were on rivers. The ever-changing water levels and the heavy traffic on the river made it difficult to work on float planes, so an amphibian would be ideal for this area. I went to Maine and met with the builder. Soon a group was formed and before the year was out the funds were raised for the second airplane for Brazil.

Then a Wycliffe translator in Brazil mentioned that there was a group from his church in Denver who were praying about raising the funds for an airplane for Brazil. I was able to arrange for a meeting with these people on the same weekend that my colleague, a JAARS pilot and author, was to speak in Denver. We flew out to Denver in a JAARS plane. I was assigned to stay with a young successful couple who drove me out to the foothills home of the people who were hosting the meeting. About twenty-five of the translator's friends were invited. We met in a large family room with windows that overlooked the city of Denver. I remember I was positioned to speak with my back to the windows—which was good for me, but I'm not sure about the audience, as the view was breathtaking.

I shared about the importance of aircraft in mission work and about the need in Brazil. I had the sinking feeling that no one was really listening, so when we took a break for coffee and doughnuts, I went out on the deck and asked God about it. "What is going on here? Why do I have this feeling that no one is listening and no one cares about this project?" About that time, one of the group, named Bob, came out on the deck and admitted, "Dave, I am really burdened about this airplane. I know that the cost will be about $50,000 and we need about $30,000 to order the plane, but I have $15,000 that I could loan to the project if that would help get it going."

I explained that the funds needed to be actually donated and that we needed the $30,000 in the project account before we could order the plane. Bob went back in and I continued asking God about what was going on—asking Him to move among the group for His glory.

A few minutes later Bob came out again and restated his proposal, "After praying about this, I have $15,000 that I will **give** to the project." I told him that I would call the JAARS director in the morning and find out about the possibility of ordering the plane considering the partial funds promised. Returning to the home of the couple who hosted me, I shared with them what Bob, a carpenter, had committed to. They surprised me by exclaiming, "We can match that." God had been working!

The next week the plane was ordered and it arrived in Brazil about six months later. God, through His people, had supplied three new aircraft for Brazil in about an eight month period. Later the JAARS director told me that had never occurred before.

Bob, an ordinary guy from Denver, inspired me by his sensitivity to the voice of God and his willingness to obey. A year or so after the meeting in Denver I was sharing with my Brazil colleague Dean, from Bob's church in Denver, how Bob, almost single handedly, was the force that provided the plane from Denver. Dean agreed, "I know."

Then Dean shared this story: "When we were in the process of applying to Wycliffe, we learned we had to attend the Summer Institute of Linguistics (SIL) at the cost of about $1300. So we saved up the money for the SIL training the following summer. Then we remembered that my wife had some school loans that had to be paid off first, so we used the money for the loans and saved up $1300 more. Something else came up that we needed the money for and so we used this money to pay a second bill. The day before we were to leave for SIL we did not have the money and did not know if we should cancel our plans and wait yet again until the funds had been raised. It was a Sunday night and we were at church praying about the problem when Bob came up to us with a check and said, 'God told me to ask if you need $1300 for something.'"

Bob's sensitivity to God's leading was contagious. Shortly thereafter, when I needed some money for an important situation in my life, Dean, unaware of the details, handed me the exact amount I needed.

―――――――

While I was in Waxhaw I learned that JAARS had serious problems sending aircraft engines to the fields where they were needed around the world. At that time an engine was worth about $10,000 and to ship one could take months. The crates they were shipped in would often disintegrate with the pounding they took and at times the engine would be damaged when it finally arrived. We learned that the U.S. military would send their engines in special steel canisters that protected the engines and sealed them from contaminant damage. Since JAARS is a charitable organization and qualified to receive surplus military material and equipment, they would often check surplus material lists for available items. When the JAARS representative stopped by a military surplus depository in Pennsylvania one day, he discovered some used canisters for shipping engines. He asked if JAARS could have one or two of them. He was told JAARS could have **all** of them. Sixteen canisters were loaded into the truck. When they arrived at JAARS, people commented how heavy they were. They were full of new engines, the same engines used on the Helio Couriers and the Hiller helicopters JAARS used around the world! For more on this story see Jamie Buckingham's book, *Into the Glory.*

———

When we first arrived in Brazil in 1969 there were five Wycliffe centers throughout the country, each separated from the other by 500 or more miles. Two aircraft, one in Porto Velho, the "Friendship of the Carolinas," and one in Belém, the "Friendship of Adrian Rogers," served the translators working out of the five centers (thus the need for three more airplanes). Adrian Rogers had been an Air Force pilot who was killed in Viet Nam. His father, Orville Rogers, was a Braniff Airline captain and had given the money from his son's life insurance to JAARS for the plane for Brazil.

After completion of the construction of the headquarters in Brasília, and the three new aircraft had arrived, I was asked to make sure that every translator who wanted and needed a tribal airstrip received the help they needed to build their airstrip. Bob Bland, of Teen Missions, promised that he could recruit teenagers to give their summers to build the airstrips needed in Brazil. Three locations were identified as viable places to send these teenagers to build needed airstrips, the Deni, the Mura–Pirahã, and the Macú. Bob recruited 100 teenagers and leaders to come to Brazil and build airstrips. He decided to charter a plane from Miami to Manaus and then transport the teenagers from there by boat to the various tribal villages.

About that time Orville Rogers was flying a Boeing 727 in and out of New York City. Just prior to take-off he noticed an alert message on the panel and requested the mechanics to check it out. They could not find the problem, but since Captain Rogers was on a time-limited schedule, and had gone past his window of take-off opportunity, another pilot had to take over. The alert message on the panel of the aircraft then disappeared. After Orville slept through the night in NYC, he was asked to pilot a charter flight from Miami to Manaus instead of the one he had missed in NYC. He accepted the opportunity. After take-off in Miami, he decided to go back to the cabin and find out why all these teenagers were going to Brazil. They exclaimed, "We are going to Brazil to build airstrips for Wycliffe Bible Translators." Orville sat down there in the cabin and cried. God had providentially given him opportunity to be part of the plan to make the ministry of the "Friendship of Adrian Rogers" even more effective.

Everyone understood that the teenagers would probably not finish any of the strips because each one needed to be nearly 2000 feet long with at least 500 feet of cleared space at each end for safety approaches. The expectation was to have the teenagers establish a beginning with the hope that the tribal people would be inspired to finish the job. Some of the areas were virgin jungle, having never been cut, but part of the proposed Deni strip was a previously cut and abandoned farm field. The teenagers and their leaders who went to the Deni village still had many large trees to cut and stumps to remove but were able to clear the stumps and fill the holes to meet the required distances. The last day of their stay in the Deni village, the WBT pilot decided to fly out and look at the airstrip. As he approached he had confidence that the airstrip was safe and landed on it. What a praise and prayer service they had right there! The teenagers were flown out of the Deni village directly to Manaus. I was given a series of slides showing the work and the challenges these teenagers endured to complete this airstrip. Whenever I shared this slide presentation in a church, I could sense that the Holy Spirit of God had touched the audience because of the hard work and sacrifice of those teenage servants.

PT-CKC and Me

6 – Flying

Oh, for wings like a dove, to fly away and rest! Psalm 55:6 (Living Bible)

Someone once said, "If God really wanted man to fly, He would have made it a lot easier to get to the airport." As a teenager I flew for the first time with Ralph Moberg, who was the father of my good friend. Ralph Moberg is a legend in my hometown, Bemidji, Minnesota. A "bush pilot's pilot," he owned Moberg Seaplane Anchorage on Lake Bemidji and would sell rides to tourists in the summer, taking off of the lake by the statues of Paul Bunyan and Babe the Blue Ox. After flying with Ralph I wanted to be a pilot. I even checked on the requirements for flying in the Air Force. Since I had astigmatism in one or both eyes, I was not qualified. I still wanted to be a pilot, but this dream was put on hold while God led me into other things.

About the time I reached forty, I realized I could never become a professional pilot. But I still wanted to learn to fly so I took a couple of weeks off one year, went back to Jungle Aviation and Radio Service headquarters, and earned my private pilot's license.

According to my flight log several Wycliffe pilots, including Harold, served as my flight instructors. Harold told me that one day when he was in Africa, he was assigned to fly cargo and passengers to a distant village. After take-off Harold realized that his alternator was not working and his battery power would soon run out. Not to worry, Harold thought, because spark for aircraft engines comes from magnetos and there are two of them on most planes. He would, however, have to spin the propeller by hand to get the plane started again once he landed in the village. After unloading his passengers and cargo and reloading for the flight back, he set the brake and the throttle and other switches at the proper setting for prop spin start; he began to turn the propeller. It did not start. Harold tried and tried to no avail. Finally the local tribal pastor asked if he wanted him to pray. Harold wished he would have thought of that and sheepishly responded, "Please." The pastor prayed and Harold tried again. This time the engine started right off. "Lord, teach us to pray!"

After I completed my pilot's training, we were assigned to the International Linguistic Center in Dallas to help raise funds for the development of the center. We attended the

Nazarene Church in Duncanville. The pastor was not only a pilot, but owned his own airplane, so pilot wannabes seemed to migrate to his church. He found five of us who wanted to fly and helped us buy a Beechcraft Musketeer. It turned out that only two of the five fellows ended up actually owning the plane. Since I could not afford more than one share, my partner owned the other four, but did not yet have a license. It was like the plane was mine alone! One day I had trouble keeping it running and I discovered that the problem was the engine-driven fuel pump. I found a shop in Dallas that would refurbish these parts. When I brought the fuel pump into him the mechanic said, "Last time I saw this fuel pump, I told the guy it would not last." Apparently the former owner had not wanted to put a lot of money into repairing or replacing the part so had sold the plane and the problem to us. It's good to find out things like this before you take off! When I returned to Brazil my partner bought me out also; he had just passed his flight test.

Back in Brazil, as soon as I could, I took my flying test in Portuguese and passed! Student pilots are told that for every hour of flight time they get two hours to talk about it, and so I took every opportunity to fly that I could possibly afford to take. When my friend, Presbyterian missionary Al Reasoner, had room and I was available, he would ask me to go with him, he acting as instructor-pilot and letting me fly left seat.

One day I was flying with Al from Anápolis to Brasília, about 100 miles. Nearing Brasília, we would call the approach control and enter the Brasília Terminal Control Area under their control. This day there was a cloud in front of us and

Instrument Flying

Licensed private pilots are required to fly under Visual Flight Rules (VFR) unless they receive extra training in instrument flying and become Instrument Flight Rules (IFR) qualified. Instruments, if relied upon, will indicate where you are, even if you can not see the ground or do not recognize the area you are flying over. VFR pilots must learn some instrument flying procedures in the dreaded case when they find themselves unable to see the ground or the horizon.

I could not see Brasília—usually visible from miles away—or the airport. The number of Al's plane was PT-CKC and when we would call the approach control or the tower, we would say "Charlie–Kilo–Charlie" or just "Charlie." This day I called, "Brasília Approach, Charlie–Kilo–Charlie, inbound, with the information." Approach's response was, "Roger, Charlie, turn left to 030." I responded, "Charlie turning left to 030." I was on a direct heading for Brasília, why would I have to turn left? (Neither Al nor I were instrument qualified.) I flew for about a minute and understood as I passed the cloud bank and Brasília and the airport came into view. As he vectored me right to a straight-in approach to the runway, I reminded myself that sometimes others (especially God) know more than I do and I need to follow their leading. As one WBT pilot reminded me—there are 100,000 parts in an approved aircraft avionics package and any one can go bad when it's needed most—yet, we trust them all implicitly. We have one God who has never failed—do we trust Him?

While our children were in college we lived in the U.S. and I took a position in Tallahassee as Manager of Airport Engineering for the Florida Department of Transportation. It was an ideal job for me because I was able to fly the State airplane to inspect projects and airports. One day I was in south Florida with a colleague I had picked up in Lakeland. It was mid-afternoon and I had a three-hour flight back to Tallahassee and wanted to get started. I called flight service weather and was told that there was a severe storm between Labelle, where I was, and Tallahassee, and was advised to wait a little while. So we had a cup of coffee and I called again. This time the advisor was a little more accommodating and said there were bad areas between Labelle and Lakeland but he thought I could pick my way around the storms.

We took off and had little trouble reaching Lakeland. Just north of Lakeland was a dark, dark cloud with lots of lightning shooting out from it. We landed and I dropped off my colleague and took off again, flying straight west for about ten minutes and, since I was west of the black cloud, turned north again. The ceiling was about 2500 feet so I was flying at 2000. When I got close to Gainesville, about halfway home, there was what looked like a curtain of rain clouds all the way across the state. Since I am just a "fair weather pilot," without an instrument license, I want to stay out of the clouds. To the left of my heading I saw what looked to me like a little "mouse hole" in the curtain of clouds and through it I could see the gulf coast and the evening sun shining on it. I thought, "It might be clear on the other side, so why not try going through?" I dropped down to about 1500 and went through.

On the other side, the clouds seemed to close in around me, enveloping the aircraft. I looked back and could not see even the "mouse hole." I knew there was an airport, Cross City, about ten miles north, so I turned north and looked. And then I saw it—flash—flash—the Cross City Airport beacon flashing through the clouds and rain! I headed toward the flashing and in about three minutes popped out of the clouds and there was the airport! I landed safely. The interesting part of the story is that the beacon was one of our department's projects and had been installed just the week before. It was there to guide me to safety. There are people out there, lost and in trouble spiritually, looking for a light to show them the way and guide them to safety. We should always do like the Lord Jesus admonished, "Let your light shine."

Another time I was alone in south Florida—Naples, on the gulf coast—and needed to look at a project in Melbourne, across the state. This time the weather was beautiful in the "Sunshine State." As one approaches Melbourne, under visual flight rules, above 2000 feet, the chart reminds the pilot to "contact Patrick Air Force Base Approach on 121.1 within twenty miles of Melbourne." About twenty-five miles out I called Patrick Approach. He gave me a transponder code to squawk and he came back and told me that I was too far out and to call him in five minutes. Five minutes later he was very busy and did not respond. I tried again and the same thing—no response. About that time I was on a ten-mile final to runway 04 at Melbourne and below 2000 feet, so I called Melbourne tower. He also was very busy and did not respond. I tried again and no response. I began to fear that my radio was receiving but not transmitting. Have you ever felt like that as you pray? It seems like you keep praying and nobody is hearing? I tried one more time. The controller must have heard the panic in my voice because he cleared me to land immediately.

———————

Down on the gulf coast, south of Tallahassee, there is a small quiet airport in a town called Carrabelle. There is also a nice southern restaurant that will have someone pick you up at the airport—about a mile away—if you call ahead. One Mother's Day our son Steven and I decided it would be fun to call ahead to the restaurant in Carrabelle and take his mom out for a special Mother's Day dinner. We reserved the plane and called the restaurant. They would be happy to pick us up—just fly over and gun the engine at about 500 feet. No problem, the weather was fine. We flew over and gunned the engine about the time we had told them that we would be there and went back to the airport and landed, taxied to the ramp, and tied down the plane. No one appeared. There were no cell phones in those days so we started walking. Delores was in her high-heeled shoes. Still no one from the restaurant came, but someone else saw us walking, picked us up, and drove us to the restaurant. We had a nice dinner and asked the manager for a ride back to the airport. He apologized profusely and drove us back. After he left we discovered that the plane's battery was dead and it would not start. We had to walk back to the restaurant and call the Tallahassee Aviation Service who had rented the plane to us. In about an hour they arrived with a fresh battery and we flew back home. Another adventure to remember.

When I was heading up the Christian Businessmen's Committee in Tallahassee, I invited a businessman from Tampa to speak at our Friday lunch. He was a pilot and flew his own plane to the lunch meeting that day. After I introduced him he began with this story. On departure from Tampa he climbed out to about 2000 feet and looked across the state toward Cape Canaveral, where the shuttle was just taking off and rocketing into space. That was a very exciting moment for him and he had to tell someone. So he got on the radio to Departure Control: "Tampa Departure, Cessna 8 Sierra Whiskey has just witnessed the take-off of the shuttle from Cape Canaveral." The controller responded, "Roger, 8 Sierra Whiskey. Maintain **visual** separation." There are some controllers with a good sense of humor.

Briefing CENTCOM Engineers on Helipads

7 – The First Gulf War

The race is not to the swift, Nor the battle to the strong, Nor bread to the wise, Nor riches to men of understanding, Nor favor to men of skill; But time

and chance happen to them all. Ecclesiastes 9:11

(New King James Bible)

Whith our daughter Valerie graduated from high school in Brazil, we felt that God would have us return to the U.S. to see our children through college. Another reason I wanted to be in the U.S. was that I had somewhat neglected my duty in the Naval Reserve and wanted to get back active and see if I could finish out my time to earn some retirement. Sadly however, after twenty years of commissioned service in the Navy Reserve, I was retired without benefits. I checked out the Army Reserve and was accepted as enlisted to earn the retirement points needed to retire with a small pension when I would reach age sixty. Being active in the Reserve has many benefits and a few risks.

When Saddam invaded Kuwait, in August, 1990, I was told that my unit, the 416th ENCOM (Engineer Command), would be called up. We were also told there were four different scenarios as to how we would be called—twenty-five could be called, forty could be called, seventy-five could be called, or the whole unit could be called. They advised, "Dave you're on every list." (I thought—what was an old gray-haired soldier in his fifties going to do?) I was the only airport engineer in the unit and they needed that expertise. Everyone was very supportive—my family, our church, the Florida Department of Transportation, and the country, in general.

We, the "Forward Detachment" of twenty-five, landed in Dhahran, Saudi Arabia, a port city with a large air base, and camped out in a couple of places, but enjoyed a temporary office building, off base, across from the U.S. Army Corps of Engineers headquarters. U.S. Army helicopter units were arriving almost daily and each commander wanted a different type of heliport for his helicopters. I think I designed thirteen different helicopter bases, some of which were constructed and others not needed. I remember one really neat "Hot Refueling Complex" I designed where helicopters could land and refuel without shutting down and remain free from desert dust. (After the war I appreciated the opportunity to go back and see it constructed. An Army transportation unit was using the concrete landing pads. There they were, just as I had designed them, but with trucks rather than helicopters.)

On Christmas Day I was transferred to King Khalid Military City, Saudi Arabia, (KKMC) a beautiful and elaborate new military base about fifty miles from the Kuwait-Iraqi border.

It was constructed in the middle of the desert and had lots of room for UN forces to assemble. (It reminded me of an extravagant and ornate movie set with lots of marble floors and high ornamental ceilings.) Our office was located in the new Engineering School (not yet occupied) right next to a Czechoslovakian chemical warfare detachment. (To think that the year before they had been our enemies behind the Iron Curtain and now they were our allies.) One day the Czechs ran into our office yelling, "Gas—Gas—Mustard

Gas." We quickly put on our gas masks and protective suits.
Our unit's chemical warfare expert, from Riyadh, was there
that day and began checking for gas but could not detect
very much. The Czech detection equipment was that much
more sensitive than ours.

———————

Besides helicopter base design, at KKMC I was involved
with locating and installing quick set-up buildings such as
K-Span steel arch buildings and Sprung Structures steel
arch and fabric buildings, as well as designing roads and
other structures. During January the UN military units were
preparing to invade Kuwait and take casualties and had
set up MASH units and even a morgue, made of sprayed
Styrofoam, with refrigeration equipment to keep it cool.

One day at about 8 a.m. the colonel came over and said,
"Dave, the major has been trying for days to prepare the site
for the crew that is coming today to put up the helicopter
hangar at the hospital. Can you help him?" The first require-

ment was a piece of earth-moving equipment that could smooth out the desert where the hangar was to be erected. The major had requested the Army heavy equipment company to help us, but they were so busy with their own projects that there was no way they could help. I went over there anyway and asked again. "No way!" was the answer. Just a block or two from the hangar site was a U.S. Air Force "Tent City." I had seen a large front-end loader operating on their roads and parking areas. If the Air Force loader were available, it would take that operator just a few minutes to clean and level a spot for the hangar.

I stopped at the Air Force security gate and asked to see the officer responsible for the front-end loader working a few hundred feet from the gate. The guard went in the "guard shack," called, and came back out with the answer I had heard many times, "Not available, come back later." I needed to talk to someone **now** and since I was already inside the gate, decided to go over and talk to the front-end loader operator myself. As I drove off, I heard the guard set off the alarm. I was talking to the operator when an officer (the captain who was "not available") drove up, with the air police. He told the police that he would take care of the situation and the police left. The captain took me back to his office and there on the wall were several large blueprints that I had made for them with our blueprint machine. I looked around and commented, "I recognize those prints—did you have them made at the Army engineers office?" In just a few minutes, the front-end loader was at the MASH area leveling off the hangar site, just as the Sprung Structure set-up crew arrived.

The next problem was the forty-eight one-meter-long pieces of half-inch steel reinforcing rod (rebar) that were needed to "nail" the framework feet to the desert floor. Behind our temporary barracks was a construction site where I had seen some lengths of rebar stored. I thought I would go over and see if I could make someone understand that I needed eight pieces cut up into one-meter lengths. Fortunately many Saudis understand and speak a little English. I found someone that seemed to be in charge and made my request. "Come back at 9 a.m. and I'll have them cut for you." Before coffee break, I had the colonel's problem solved and was back at my own work. I took the rest of the morning off and wrote a long letter to my wife, Delores, telling the whole story that I felt was a series of blessed miracles from God.

———————

Early one morning in February the colonel again came up and said urgently, "An A-10 just crashed on the runway. Go over and assess the damage and see what is needed to repair it." I went over to the airport and found the airport manager, a U.S. Air Force captain, told him who I was, and what I had been asked to do. He said, "Okay. Let's go look at it." We got into his "jeep," a two-door Ford Bronco, the kind with the spare tire on the back, and drove to the end of the runway. The A-10 was still there, upside down, just off the runway on the infield. It broke my heart, we had lost the pilot. The captain stopped his "jeep" near the plane and sighed, "It's been a hard day."

The A-10 (Warthog) is a small bomber that also fires air-to-ground missiles. It is slow for a jet, but quite maneuverable and was used extensively in this war. I asked, "Did you see it happen?" It had been hit over Iraq, but still flyable, though without total control. The pilot thought he could come in a little fast and land safely. "Yes," he admitted, "I was right here." When the pilot had cut the power to touch down, the right wheel had struck the approach and flipped him over and come right at the captain and his "jeep." I looked around. The back window was broken out and the spare tire was in shreds. "He hit you?" "Yes," he repeated, trying to keep from crying and laying his head on the steering wheel, "It's been a hard day."

All military personnel in the war zone were provided a security clearance — usually "confidential," "secret," or "top secret." There were many "top secret" issues I did not want to know about and tried to keep from those briefings as much as possible. But one day near the end of February I was summoned to a briefing for everyone who had a "top secret" clearance. The briefer told us that our UN commanders had decided to invade Kuwait that night and outlined their plans for accomplishing the invasion. After the briefing I went back to work. In a few minutes I was called to the phone. It was my wife, Delores, who exclaimed, "I hear you are going in tonight." "That is top secret, so how do you know?" It was on CNN!

———————

After the Iraqi Army left Kuwait, the U.S. Army engineers were asked to go to Kuwait and assess the damage. The first day in Kuwait City we were allowed to just drive around and talk to the people. Everywhere we went we were thanked with tears and stories of the terrible things the Iraqis had done while they were there. Then each morning we were given a few critical places to inspect, report on the damage, and estimate repairs required and/or equipment needed. The commanders were especially concerned about clinics, supermarkets, and water supply facilities.

One day we were sent to a supermarket that had obviously been closed since before the occupation. It was my turn to make the inspection and write the report. The store had been closed for some time, windows were boarded over and the emergency generator had not been used. We parked near the front of the store and the rest of the parking lot was empty. As I sat there writing the report I noticed an Arab man, dressed in the typical Arab long flowing robe with a covering scarf on his head, walking on the far side of the parking lot. At the same time he noticed us and began a determined advance to our vehicle. I was sitting in the passenger's side, and the colonel in the driver's seat. When the man arrived, it was apparent that he did not speak English, but wanted desperately to communicate. So he placed his hands on his heart and then extended them to us as though he were offering his heart to us. Then he placed his hands on his head and again extended them to us. Finally he placed his hands together as if in a prayer and again extended them to us. With tears streaming down his face, he then turned around and walked back to the other side of the parking lot. That day, if there were any doubts about the U.S. involvement in Desert Storm, they were completely erased. God had confirmed in my mind that the U.S. had done the right thing.

Another day we were assigned to inspect several clinics. These clinics were open, but unless they had their own emergency power supply, they did not have electricity or water. Wells drilled in Kuwait yield oil, so water must be pumped from the sea and the salt removed in order for it to be used for general consumption. The Iraqis had left the water system in shambles so water had to be brought in by truck and rationed. We wanted to make sure the clinics had emergency power and potable water available.

The first clinic we visited that day was headed by a Palestinian doctor. His story reminded me of the plight of Palestinians and other foreigners in Middle Eastern countries. He told us how he was treated like a foreigner in Kuwait. In fact, he felt his sons studying in the United States were treated more like citizens than he was. Further, since many of the clinical workers were from other countries, and not Kuwait, he wanted to communicate with them. He was afraid that the Kuwaiti government, now that they were free to take over again, might punish some of the foreigners who they thought may have collaborated with the Iraqis. He mentioned he knew of several other clinics that he could take us to that also needed to be inspected and provided with electricity and water. Under the existing martial law restrictions, he could not get to these clinics on his own, so he asked us to take him under the pretense that he was showing us where these other clinics were. We took him around—he was able to communicate with his colleagues (in Arabic) and we were able to get a report on the other clinics' status regarding electricity and water.

Finally, after a week of inspections, the damage assessment coordinators had run out of places that needed inspecting. On this day they asked us to inspect a super-market that we had tried to find previously but could not find (we thought it had been torn down), so we looked for it one more time. When we could not find it, I suggested that we go for a ride out of town toward the Iraqi border and see if we could reach the Euphrates River, about seventy miles north. After driving for almost an hour, we spotted two guys crawling out in the desert yelling and waving. The colonel stopped and said, "Maybe they are Iraqis. Let's get them. Dave, you stay here and cover us, and the lieutenant and I will go get them." The men looked like they needed help, but it could have been an ambush. We always carried our weapon, an M-16 automatic rifle, our flack jacket, and helmet, but did not always have it all ready. I carried a belt that had on it two cartridge magazine pockets, each holding two magazines. Each magazine held 20 rounds but since a magazine with 20 rounds was quite heavy, I used one pocket for my camera and the other pocket had one magazine with rounds and the other magazine was empty.

I reached into the pocket that had the magazines and pulled one out. It was the empty one. I pulled out the other and rammed it home in the M-16. It fell out on the highway pavement. I said out loud, "Dave, what are you doing here?" and started to laugh. The colonel wondered what was happening—but I recovered. We discovered our prisoners were Iraqi solders assigned to a silkworm missile site which coalition forces had bombed, killing four of their colleagues. They hated Saddam. Having not eaten for over four days, they devoured everything we gave them from our emergency supply and were very happy that we had come along and saved their lives. We turned them over to a British hospital and went back to our temporary barracks. We were the only engineers who "took prisoners" in this war.

Almost two years after the war I was assigned to the section of the 416th ENCOM which dealt with mobilization of the unit's engineers and met monthly at Fort McPherson in Atlanta. Since I lived in Tallahassee, and it was a four-hour drive to Atlanta, I had to leave home at 4 a.m. The weather forecast for the March drill weekend was not good, and when I left that morning, what was later called the "Storm of the Century" was blowing across the south and predicted to churn up the east coast over the weekend. I noticed as I left Tallahassee that the wind was blowing hard and leaves and branches were all over the road. Snow flurries were in the air. The weather report on the radio said that the storm would not reach Atlanta until 9 a.m. and I felt I would arrive there before that time.

There was hardly any traffic but about twenty minutes north of Tallahassee I noticed a car approaching. Then suddenly its headlights disappeared—and then I saw it—a large tree across the highway. I was going 55 mph with no way to stop in time. I said, "Lord, this is it, here I come." I heard two big thumps—one when the car hit the tree and the other when my head hit the steering wheel. I sat up and said to myself, "I'm still alive—I better get out of here." I was able to get the seatbelt unbuckled and the door opened, but when I got to the rear wheel I passed out on the pavement. When I woke up there was a lady beside me praying in tongues. She helped me up, sat me on the tree trunk, said the ambulance was on its way, and left.

I was bleeding badly between my eyes where I had hit the steering wheel. My collar bone was broken from the seatbelt, my knees were bruised, and some bones in my hands were broken. When the ambulance got me to the emergency room the doctor on duty was a plastic surgeon and she sewed up the cut between my eyes so that no scar can be seen today. I asked her if I could tell my friends I had a "nose job" by a plastic surgeon. She did not think it was funny, but later when I mentioned that to a friend, he looked at it closely and said, "It's still swollen, isn't it?"

Shortly after I got to the hospital my pastor arrived and prayed with me. The storm was so bad that the police would not let Delores drive to the hospital. She was finally able to make it a few hours later and I stayed in the hospital for two days. God is good. It's been nearly fifteen years now and I have suffered no serious aftereffects.

Brazil Christian Military Conference

8 – Entertaining Angels

Do not forget to entertain strangers, for by so doing some have unwittingly entertained angels. Hebrews 13:2 (New King James Bible)

When I was in Naval Officer Candidate School (OCS), the Officers Christian Fellowship group met at the home of an Army colonel. When it came time for graduation, he invited my parents to stay in his home while they visited for the graduation ceremony. I inquired, "How can I repay you?" He replied, "You can't repay me but you can do the same for others and what goes around, comes around." Entertain often enough and you will be entertaining angels without knowing it.

———

The Military Christian Fellowship became very important to me, not only at OCS, but also during my active duty in New Orleans. So when I arrived in Brazil, I tried to find a similar group. The international organization told me of a Navy dentist in Rio and a cadet in the military academy who were working to establish a Christian military organization in Brazil. In Rio I met the dentist and found that he had a good group participating there, but since I lived 1000 miles away in Brasília, I really could not join them. The cadet, however, had just graduated and was being assigned to Brasília. Cadet Pablo became a dear friend as we worked together to initiate the group in Brasília and help the groups on other bases begin meeting. Soon others took leadership and the organization began to grow. The Brazil association is now said to be the largest Christian military organization in the world.

It was amazing to me to watch the men as they came together, especially the first-timers. They did not know what to expect—junior officers meeting with those of higher rank and Army officers meeting with officers from the Air Force, Navy, or Marine Corps. Then, with tears, they would share what it meant to be able to experience the warm and supportive fellowship of other Christian military officers.

When U.S. Army General Bob was assigned to be U.S. military attaché, he wanted to be involved with the Brazilian Christian military group. His enthusiasm encouraged many of the participants, not only the Brazilians, but also attachés from other countries. One day a Brazilian Army unit was on maneuvers in the field and invited General Bob to come out

and inspect the troops. As he was being introduced to the officers he went down the line, from higher rank to lower rank,
shaking their hands and greeting them. At the junior officer
end was Lt. Pablo, whom the general knew well but was
surprised to see with this unit. Instead of greeting him with
the usual, "Good to meet you, lieutenant," he said, "Brother
Pablo" and gave him a big Brazilian "*abraço*" (bear hug).
The others could not believe what they were seeing. Pablo
had a lot of explaining to do—that this was a common practice among Christians, even military officers.

When we first arrived in Brazil we heard of a service the
Air Force provided people in the rural areas, called "National
Air Mail Service." The Air Force would fly the mail between
rural towns and the big cities, and would give rides to passengers as well. The service was like the proverbial "milk run"
in that it would stop often and take all day to go where mail
and passengers needed to go. But since it was free or almost

free, I used the service on occasion. I remember one trip from Belém back to Brasília; I was riding with the pilot, a major named Rollapiano. (Not his real name, but what comes to my mind when I think of him.) The trip was uneventful, but I did not forget the name.

A few years later, when my dad was dying of cancer, I was called home to be with him. We were living in Porto Velho at the time, and I bought a ticket out of Manaus to the U.S. with a connecting leg from Porto Velho to Manaus the day before, a Sunday. We were at the Porto Velho airport and the plane arrived, but for some reason they could not refuel. While we were waiting I noticed an Air Force general there, also waiting, and went up to talk to him. It was Rollapiano. I reminded him that I had flown with him one time.

A little later a Brazilian Air Force C-130 landed and was refueling on its way to Manaus. The pilots came in to the waiting area, noticed that my wife and I were Americans, so talked to us to practice their English. About the time they were going to take off again I asked the pilot if he had room for me, because I had an international connection to make in Manaus and it looked like the flight I was scheduled on was not going that day. He told me I had to talk to his boss, General Rollapiano. So I went back to the general and asked if I could ride on the Air Force plane to Manaus. He approved my request so I went to the commercial agent and asked to get my checked luggage out of the plane. We went out to the plane and found my bag and I took it over to the C-130 and got on. I no sooner got strapped in than General Rollapiano also came on board and asked how I had managed to get my bag from the commercial plane. "The agent got it for me," I explained. But sadly, he had not been able to find the agent. God had provided a way for me; the general would have to wait.

When our daughter Valerie graduated from high school in Brasília and was accepted at Oak Hills Christian College, we felt that God would have us return to the United States and be closer to our children while they were in school. As we left Brasília I mentioned to Walter, a Brazilian teenager who worked at the WBT headquarters, that if he ever wanted to come to the United States he should call us because we had a place for him. Walter Soares, son of a Brazilian missionary nurse, grew up on the Kaiwá Indian Mission, together with the children of Wycliffe missionaries John and Audrey. Before starting high school he had asked if he could come to Brasília, live on our headquarters campus, work for the mission during the day, and study high school at night. The WBT administrative department needed help picking up and distributing the mail every day, as well as making purchases for the office. This job for Walter was the perfect arrangement for both him and WBT. We grew to love him as he was an outstanding individual in every way.

When Walter was finishing high school in Brasília, he called me and asked if the invitation was still open. It was, of course, and he came and repeated his senior year in Minnesota. For Walter to graduate from a U.S. high school, certain course requirements like U.S. and Minnesota History had to be met. Walter took all three years of English, the history courses and all the other requirements to graduate in one year and was inducted into the National Honor Society! Besides this, he was a star on the conference champion soccer team, sang in the church youth choir, ministered with the evangelism program, and worked part-time on the handicap school bus. When we would go to school for conferences with his teachers, they all said that Walter was an example and an inspiration to the American students.

In the spring of that year I was invited to participate in the Brazilian Christian Military National Conference. Since I was back in Brazil, I decided to visit some of the Wycliffe centers. On the way I was to pass through Campo Grande, where Walter's mother was living at the time. I would have about an hour at the airport and so I called her ahead of time and asked if she would come to the airport to talk with me. I was so proud of Walter and how well he was doing that I wanted to share this with his mother. I enthusiastically told her, there at the airport, all that Walter was doing and how much everyone thought of him. So it broke my heart when I looked at her and saw tears streaming down her face. When I asked what was wrong, she said, "I have already lost my son."

After that, I told Walter that he could stay with us only until graduation, so he quickly found another family to stay with while attending a community college in Illinois and then on to Western Illinois University where he graduated with a Masters in Finance. He was hired by Cargill, with headquarters in Minnesota, but was soon sent to work in Brazil and various other locations. I was surprised when he called one day from Chicago. He had met a beautiful Irish girl at Moody Church and was going to marry her. Would I be his best man? Their wedding was in Northern Ireland and Walter's mother was able to attend. One of the responsibilities of the best man in Ireland was to give a speech at the reception. I was thrilled to relate this sketch of God's powerful presence in our lives as He brought us all together. Over the years, Walter, Helen, and their daughters have spent some years in Brazil, close to his mother, who is well cared for by her successful son.

In 1977 when we were home in the U.S., the Wycliffe director asked me to help raise funds for the development of the International Linguistics Center in Dallas. While I was there that year I met a young Bible translator named Chet Bitterman, and even played some soccer with him. A couple of years later, back in Brazil, I was acting as manager of government relations, a job that required me to meet and tell our story to high ranking military officers, national congressmen, and state governors and representatives. I was on a first name basis with several national congressmen and military officials as I did my best to "entertain" them while sharing the heart and focus of our work.

March 7, 1981, was one of the lowest points of my life. That day the M-19 terrorist group killed my friend, Chet Bitterman, on a bus in Colombia. For forty-seven days we had been praying for Chet's release. The military officers in our group were praying and several said they believed God would set him free. Friends of Wycliffe around the world were praying for Chet—maybe more people were praying for him than had ever prayed for one person before—but M-19 killed him.

The following is an excerpt from the letter I wrote that day to my supporting churches and friends:

"This morning we heard that the terrorist group M-19 had killed our colleague, Wycliffe Bible Translator Chet Bitterman, in Colombia. Is it really worth it all? "Two years ago we were asked to return to Brazil to help secure a new contract with the government. We still do not have it.

"If a terrorist group in Brazil wanted to impress the government by killing a Wycliffe member, I would be a likely candidate because of my personal acquaintance with many influential people.

"Would you want a job without a fixed salary, without retirement, in a place where you can't offer your family the opportunities they deserve and by accepting the work you also accept the possibility of risking your life?

"The Lord Jesus was rejected and killed. What a privilege to spend yourself—in life or in death in service for Him—sharing His love. It's not just the Bittermans, nor the Scherlings. We are in this together. Young people are needed to take Chet's place, others to support us—prayerfully and financially, so that Chet's death will not be in vain."

———

In order to study the Indian languages in Brazil and translate the Bible into the languages, Wycliffe Bible Translators, through SIL, worked closely with the Brazilian Indian agency. Often relationships were strained and work was interrupted. So whenever the agency installed a new president, it was our hope that working relationships would improve. When we heard that a retired Army colonel was going to be inaugurated as head of the agency, we hoped for an opportunity to share our work and ask for smooth relationships. After he had been in the position a few weeks, we sought and were granted an appointment to see him and share our vision for the native people and their languages.

Our team of five top Wycliffe leaders had prepared a presentation to help him understand our heart for the people and our work. Our Wycliffe colleagues, those not going to the meeting, were spending the day in prayer for God's blessing in the endeavor. We had also shared this meeting opportunity as a prayer request with our supporters and Wycliffe members in other countries.

But, the colonel had previous experience with Americans and was expecting a "slick" American sales pitch. When we offered him a copy of the New Testament in the Hixcariana language, the first translated in Brazil, he said he could not accept it, because government officials were not allowed to accept gifts. That set the tone for the meeting so that presentations by various translators on the team were strained and when we asked him and his cabinet to come to our center for dinner and see firsthand what we do, he again refused because they could not reciprocate. The colonel had listened politely to the presentation, but did not seem to see the passion for our work in his country.

I was personally devastated. We had bathed this program in prayer for weeks—convinced that God had us in Brazil for the purpose of giving His Word to those who had never heard the gospel. Why had God abandoned us? Back at the WBT center the team came together again, and the Executive Committee Chairman and translator for a native language group in Brazil brought us to Romans 8.

[31] What can we ever say to such wonderful things as these? If God is on our side, who can ever be against us? [32] Since he did not spare even his own Son for us but gave him up for us all, won't he also surely give us everything else? [33] Who dares accuse us whom God has chosen for his own? Will God? No! He is the one who has forgiven us and given us right standing with himself. [34] Who then will condemn us? Will Christ? No! For he is the one who died for us and came back to life again for us and is sitting at the place of highest honor next to God, pleading for us there in heaven. [35] Who then can ever keep Christ's love from

us? When we have trouble or calamity, when we are hunted down or destroyed, is it because he doesn't love us anymore? And if we are hungry or penniless or in danger or threatened with death, has God deserted us? [36]No, for the Scriptures tell us that for his sake we must be ready to face death at every moment of the day—we are like sheep awaiting slaughter; [37]but despite all this, overwhelming victory is ours through Christ who loved us enough to die for us. [38]For I am convinced that nothing can ever separate us from his love. Death can't, and life can't. The angels won't, and all the powers of hell itself cannot keep God's love away. Our fears for today, our worries about tomorrow, [39]or where we are—high above the sky, or in the deepest ocean—nothing will ever be able to separate us from the love of God demonstrated by our Lord Jesus Christ when he died for us. Romans 8:31-39 (Living Bible)

A week later Bible translator Bob came to Brasília from the village where he worked, 1000 miles west, near Porto Velho. A nine-year-old native girl, Bonita, from one of the villages he served had a spinal problem and needed surgery that could be done only at a special hospital in the United States. Bob wanted to request permission from the Indian agency to take Bonita to the U.S. and have the surgery performed. We cautioned, "Don't expect a positive response—the new agency head is a hard man." Bob himself had suffered from polio as a child and walked with two canes, slowly and deliberately, and talked the same way. Undaunted, Bob, in his work clothes, proceeded with his goal. The head of the Indian agency cordially received him and granted permission to take Bonita to the U.S. God used this "unadorned" visit to impress upon the agency head that our work was important to the native people he served. Two weeks later the colonel and all his top aides came out to our center for dinner and a presentation of our work in Brazil. He became a good friend and we enjoyed a period of favorable relations.

The Johnsons and Friend

9 – Terima Kasih

Thanks be to God for His indescribable gift! II Corinthians 9:15 (New King James Bible)

When we served in Indonesia we learned a little Bahasa Indonesia, the language of Indonesia. *Terima kasih* are the words generally translated "thank you" in Indonesian. The words, however, literally mean "received love." We have received love down through the years and have enjoyed God's presence with us and especially His indescribable gift!

During our first visit to Papua (formerly Irian Jaya), Indonesia, in 1994, we landed in a village of the M speakers in the south lowlands of Papua. We were there because Ed, our son-in-law, was teaching in a small, native Bible school and we wanted to be with our granddaughters, Hannah, two and a half years old, and Elizabeth, eight months. For entertainment we would go to the river or hike along the airstrip. (This was the closest airstrip to Obukain, where our daughter and family live and work.) It was on the airstrip that I heard the incredible story of God's powerful work to bring the gospel to the M speaking people. There are churches in all the M villages, the New Testament translation has been facilitated by a dear Papuan native, and the pastors and church leaders have helped the people of Obukain and other native peoples of the area.

In 1999 while we were serving in Indonesia, M pastor Daniel was studying at the Bible school in the city where we were working. He called me one morning very distraught because his four-year-old son had fallen on the concrete and Daniel thought his arm was broken. The son was in terrible pain and Daniel was in tears—he did not know where the clinic was, could not speak much Indonesian, and he did not have transportation, other than taxi, to take his son for medical help. I promised I would come and take them to the clinic. I asked our colleagues at the center to pray and drove over to the school. The medical people at the clinic did not have access to x-ray equipment and recommended that we take the son to the next town for x-rays. The process took all morning, the son was suffering, but very trusting, and finally the results came back—no broken bones.

The New Testament is now completed in M language and the church leaders have been instigators to help in many ways the D people who live in Obukain. In fact, Pastor Daniel walked the two days, with his family, to Obukain, just to see me, the last time I visited there.

———

In 1999 I retired from the State of Florida Department of Transportation Aviation Office and began service as field administrator for the Papua, then Irian Jaya, field of World Team. The office was located in Sentani, a town which had been given a big boost during World War II when General Douglas MacArthur set up his Pacific base of operations nearby after he was forced out of the Philippine Islands. He chose that area because it was just twenty-five miles from the port town of Jayapura, was situated on the south side of the 8,000 foot Mount Cyclops, and boasted the only flat, level spot for a runway in the area between Mount Cyclops and Lake Sentani. MacArthur set up base camps on the mountainside a short distance from the runway he was building and had the U.S. Navy Seabees build a road from Jayapura to Sentani.

After the war the Christian mission groups who came to minister in the area were looking for places to establish their headquarters and were given the property called Post 7. The missionaries were thankful because concrete parking lots, Quonset huts, and even a large swimming pool were still useable. I learned this as we were being given our orientation and as we visited the places that are still preserved.

But my mind returned to an incident I had experienced twenty-two years earlier. We were in the United States on furlough from Wycliffe-Brazil, when I was asked to give the "Challenge to the Congregation" for the commissioning service for Pete, an Oak Hills Christian College graduate, friend of our family, and new member of Wycliffe-Brazil. I shared the recently published story of Carol, also an Oak Hills graduate and one of the first Wycliffe missionaries to Irian Jaya, Indonesia. When Carol and her partner first arrived in Indonesia they were given a tour of one of the other islands. From a high hill, their Indonesian guide showed them a large valley and exclaimed that in this valley was one of the bloodiest battles of World War II between the Americans and the Japanese. Then he looked at Carol and her partner—her partner was Japanese!

———

Along the center of Papua, both Papua New Guinea and Papua Indonesia, lies a high mountain range with peaks as high as 16,000 feet. Many different tribal groups live in the valleys and mountain ridges as well as on both sides of the mountain range. There are 269 different languages listed in the *Ethnologue* in Papua, Indonesia, alone. These groups live isolated from each other because of the difficulty in travel. Since World War II, missionaries and others have entered the area and travel has become better, mainly by aircraft. However, it is still very difficult to get around.

While we were in Obukain visiting a few years ago, our granddaughter Elizabeth came down with malaria. Even though her dad, Ed, has been an EMT and treats the village population medically, the treatment he had administered was not affecting Elizabeth's fever. At a certain time every morning the medical doctor came on the radio and answered the questions of missionaries and others who might be listening. So Ed called the doctor and asked about another treatment for Elizabeth. The doctor replied, "Yes, there is another treatment and I have some right here. There just happens to be an aircraft here right now and I will give it to the pilot to take to the aviation center in Wamena."

We were expecting a plane from Wamena to pick us up that day. Ed called the aviation center and asked the pilot if he could wait for the medicine to arrive before he took off. He agreed and in a couple of hours the plane arrived with the medicine, and with treatment Elizabeth was fine the next day.

Late one night in Obukain, Ed and Valerie were disturbed by what sounded like a riot in the village. Such disturbances had happened before and it is expedient for Ed and Valerie to get over to the village as soon as possible. First it is just shouting—then certain villagers grab sticks or long poles from the jungle and threaten one another with them—and then out come the machetes and other weapons. Ed and Valerie missed the timing on this occasion, however, because soon there was shouting at their door and a young man was there with a machete wound down his chest. Ed had done some suturing before (without the benefit of anesthetic), but this fellow had already lost a lot of blood and was soon to lose consciousness.

Calling the doctor was not an option since he monitored his radio only during the day, and Ed needed advice right away. Valerie's brother's wife, Toni, back in Minnesota, is a nurse and it was daytime there. So Ed called her on the satellite phone. We happened to be with Bill and Toni that day. Delores was in the downstairs bedroom when she heard Toni on the phone so she went upstairs to see if she could help with the girls. She realized that it was Ed on the phone with Toni and that there was an emergency in Obukain. Not only did Ed need Toni's encouragement in the suturing—they discussed the appropriateness of suturing to minimize the infection—but the young man was in desperate need of some fluid. Ed had one bag of IV "drip" but he had never hooked anyone up to IV fluids and needed advice on how to insert the needle into the vein. Toni was able to give him step-by-step instructions on how to start the IV and how to help keep the wound free from infection. Colleagues spread the word around to praying friends and relatives and the young man's life was saved. He healed very quickly and is now a leader among the Diuwe youth.

In 2006 Ed's brother and some others, including myself, flew into Obukain to help put the finishing touches on Valerie and Ed's new house. We flew in with our Wycliffe pilot friends and as the pilots were inspecting the airstrip, as they are required to do every so often, a pig ran out and crossed the airstrip. Pigs and aircraft do not make good airstrip companions, so the pilots are required to kill the pig. The pig could not be found so the people of the village were left to kill the pig later. The owner of the pig is a rather independent fellow, and the village people, in general, do not react very rapidly to situations like this. It was Ed's opinion that we might not be able to keep our return-to-the-U.S. reservations because they were in three weeks and the decision to kill the pig would take longer than that.

We were quite surprised and relieved when the village leaders and the owner of the pig came over the next day and said they would kill the pig. Our granddaughters were flying in for the weekend and the dead pig would be given to the pilot who brought them. When they came in, the dead pig was there and the pilot took home some fresh pig legs. Just another "never-before" happening in the lives of the Lord's servants.

———————

Earlier in 2006 Delores and I had traveled to Obukain with our son Steven and a home-builder friend, Troy, and his daughter, Tori. We were there to frame up the new house but had only five and a half days to do it. Yet, when we left, the walls were up and the rafters had a good start. Ed and Valerie were pleased. There were a couple of minor miracles that are worth repeating.

For electricity Ed had a generator that he would start up when we needed power tools, which was most of the working hours we were there. One day near the end of our time in Obukain, Troy needed a power saw on the second-story floor joists and asked for one. One of the local fellows understood what he was asking for and reached down to pick it up. He picked it up by the handle, but in doing so, squeezed the trigger and the saw started. With his other hand he reached for the blade to stop it. I watched in horror as this all unfolded, and thought, "This is not good!" Fortunately, the blade guard was in place and he did not get hurt, just a little surprised, as we all were.

Tori was twelve at the time and wore cute little glasses even when she went down to the river for a swim and to bathe. I don't know if she set her glasses on a dug-out canoe, or if they came off in the current, but she lost her glasses in the river. The young boys of Obukain fish with slingshots and tiny metal spears by swimming underwater, finding a fish, and shooting the little spear. They are very observant and accurate. So Ed called a couple of little guys and told them that Tori had lost her glasses in the fast river current, and within just a few minutes one of them came up with her glasses. She was delighted and thankful to see well again.

While we were in Papua we met a number of really extraordinary missionaries from different missions and denominations. Bud is one of them. The tribal village where he worked is located near the southern edge of the high mountain range not far from the commercial and aviation center of Wamena. One day during our time there an Indonesian Air Force plane was trying to fly across the high part of the mountain range in the clouds and hit the side of the mountain. Everyone on board was killed. The accident occurred not too far from Bud's village. The Air Force brought in some planes to hunt for the wreckage and try to retrieve the bodies. They worked for several days but did not find the wreckage. Finally the officer in charge (a member of the majority religion) asked Bud if the medicine man could work out some magic to help them find the downed plane and crew. Bud said, "No, I don't think so but he does know the God of creation and will be happy to talk to Him for you."

The chief prayed in his own language and sent the Air Force off to look again. In a few minutes they were back with the report that they had found the wreckage and could reach it soon with the helicopter.

The highlight of our time in Papua was when we attended dedications of New Testaments in the languages of the people. So when we were invited to participate in the dedication of the N New Testament, we did not hesitate. N land is in the high mountain region, south and east of the central city of Wamena. There are no roads and it is a four-day walk from Wamena, so most of the visitors came in small planes. There were seven planes at the high end of the airstrip when we landed.

As I walked to the dedication area of the village, I met a gray-haired man about my age. I greeted him, "Hi, who are you?" He explained, "My name is Stan. I was the first white man to walk over these mountains and reach this valley. Older fellows from the village still remember me. They said that when I first came they were going to kill me and eat me, but I started to work on the airstrip and they decided to let me live. I worked here for seven years—buried my infant son right over there—and finally had to leave because of my wife's health. I just retired from thirty-five years as a pastor in Toronto."

As we enjoyed the dedication, we learned more about how God had worked in this language group. After Stan had left, another missionary came and began translating the Gospel of Mark. In a few years, finally one man accepted the Lord. He would go from hut to hut every day and say, "Come and hear the Word of God. Come and hear the Word of God."

During the dedication ceremony we watched the people dramatize the change that had occurred, from warring and cannibalizing, to learning and studying the Scriptures. In the audience, seated behind the visitors, were about fifty young Bible school students dressed in white shirts and black pants. The rest of the people sat in the natural amphitheater around the main speaker's platform. Several officials spoke, including the governor of the state. Finally came the time for the New Testament to be distributed. The first person to be given the New Testament was the evangelist who had first accepted the Lord and labored for years to evangelize the rest of the people. When he walked up to receive his New Testament, all the people jumped up and shouted, in honor of this evangelist. (Chills went up and down my spine and still do today as I am writing this.) God was also cheering; and as I looked at the evangelist's ugly and gnarled feet, from years of hiking rocky mountain trails, I was reminded of Isaiah 52:7.

How beautiful upon the mountains are the feet of him who brings good news. (New King James Bible)

Today there are thirty-five churches in that valley and the surrounding area. Bible students there in the village are working on the translation of the Old Testament in the N language and have recently published a children's version in their language. The work is being done on laptop computer and e-mailed by radio to the translation consultants for review and revision.

Belem—Brasília Highway, 1969

10 – Does God Provide?

And my God shall supply all your need according to
His riches in glory by Christ Jesus. Philippians 4:19
(New King James Bible)

We spent our first month in Brazil at Belém, at the
mouth of the Amazon River, while we waited for

our shipment of barrels to arrive by boat. Our international plane tickets continued from Belém to Brasília. When our shipment came, the Belém Wycliffe manager found a truck to take the boxes and barrels to Brasília. I had heard about the Belém-Brasília highway (1200 miles recently cut through the jungle) and really wanted to see and experience the road trip, so I asked the manager to find out if I could ride along with the shipment. That was approved and another Bible translator was able to use my air ticket.

Finally the day came when the truck driver came to pick up the shipment, and me, to make the four-day trip. One other passenger rode the first day and I sat in between them. They spoke only Portuguese and I knew a little Spanish but could not really understand everything they said or communicate with them. The road was fine until we reached the edge of town. In the countryside the road was only a bulldozer-cut through the jungle without any pavement structure to speak of. Since it rains about ten feet a year in the Amazon, the subgrade was not only wet, but muddy, and in places the ruts were deeper than the truck could manage. Early on I noticed that the driver was not able to shift up higher than second or third gear, so we were not traveling very fast.

We would stop at places along the road where we could buy something to eat, and then late at night we would stop at a *pensão*, a small place to sleep like an inn or a boarding house. I remember one of the first evenings we stopped at a small "restaurant"—a place with adobe walls, a thatched roof, and tables. We walked in and sat at a table. The young waitress came over and looked at me. I looked at the driver who said in Portuguese, "He'll have supper and I'll have supper." She asked, "Doesn't he speak Portuguese?" The driver replied, "No, he doesn't speak anything." "Where is he from?" she asked. "From Portugal," he replied. They both laughed. It wasn't until later I learned that some Brazilians think that the dumbest people in the world are from Portugal—so dumb, like me, they can't speak Portuguese.

One of the things that scared me when I thought about going on this trip was where would I go to the bathroom? I specifically asked God to provide a way for me in this regard.

He answered and I was constipated the whole way—not sick or hurting—just never had to go.

After three days I had come to the place where it was not fun any more. Portuguese all day everyday and no one to talk to in my own language; sleeping was a challenge because I had to share my room with more than the driver—mice and bats and dogs and cats, as well as some farm animals. To keep from sharing my snacks with them, this particular night I hung my bag on a cord strung from one rafter to the other. Still I woke up often hearing scampering along the room divider and over the roof joists. Sleep was sparse and I was awake early in the morning when someone with an accordion, seemingly in the next room, began to play. It was a hymn—one that I knew and sang along in English.

"Alas and did my Savior bleed and did my Sov'reign die?

Would He devote that sacred head for such a worm as I?

At the cross, at the cross, where I first saw the light

And the burden of my heart rolled away—

It was there by faith I received my sight,

And now I am happy all the day."

Just one time through—and that is all there was—but God had provided enough to get me back on track and remember why I was there.

During our second term in Brazil I was assigned to help with government relations, that is, to try to keep our real work in the minds of those in power and not the half-truths that our enemies continually bombarded them with. At that time one of our colleagues who had worked in several Latin American countries suggested that we invite Rosita, a society lady from Lima, Peru, and well-known throughout Latin America, to come and share with some of her friends in Brazil about the work of Wycliffe around the world. Rosita was a good friend and had promoted the work very successfully in other countries. She gladly accepted our invitation and worked hard on our behalf for several weeks.

While she was in Brazil, an old friend of hers, the president of the Supreme Court of the Lima area, came to spend a few days. We became friends and he confided that one thing that he would really love to do would be to meet and have an interview with the president of the Supreme Court of Brazil. Emmit Young, Presbyterian missionary and dear friend, was chaplain of the Brazil National Congress and led Bible studies in several high government offices. The Supreme Court chief of staff was a member of one of those Bible studies. I asked Emmit if he would introduce the Peruvian judge to his friend in the Supreme Court and see if we could help him fulfill his dream. I remember the day because I drove him and Emmit to the Supreme Court Building for their appointment with the president of the Supreme Court of Brazil. When the Peruvian judge came out, about an hour later, he was on "cloud nine" and told Emmit that if he ever came to Lima to be sure to look him up at any time.

About a year later Emmit, in his leadership responsibilities with congressional chaplains in other countries, went to Peru to encourage Bible studies in every level of the government. After he completed his agenda, he remembered the words of the Peruvian judge and went to the Supreme Court Building to see if he was available. Emmit went in and asked the receptionist if the judge, president of the Supreme Court, was in. She told him that the judge was in court at that moment and not available. Emmit asked if she would call up to the judge's office and tell him that Emmit Young from Brazil was in the foyer. She did and the judge sent word down for Emmit to come up to the court room. Emmit said that when he opened the door, and the judge saw that it was he, the judge stood up and announced, "This court is in recess for a few minutes," and motioned for Emmit to meet him in his chambers. After about an hour of chatting and praying Emmit said, "Is the court still waiting for you?" "Yes," he said, "I better get back in there."

Emmit was a spiritual blessing to the judge. The judge was an encouragement to those active in the Bible studies in the government offices of Peru. The hand of God was evident.

————————

Wycliffe Bible Translators is a "faith" mission, that is, each missionary must raise their own financial support. (This money is given to the mission, which, in turn, uses it to pay the missionary's salary.) Every month we would get a computer printout that listed which churches and individuals had given and the amount they gave. This report helped us with our responsibility to thank the donors and the Lord. At one period during our time in Brazil, I noticed that a retired widow lady named Lilly White, a dear friend of my mother's, was giving more and more. This was a source of consternation for me because I knew her situation, and we lived in a much nicer place than she did.

Finally we had our chance to return to the U.S. and we looked her up to thank her personally. I told her we noticed that she was giving more and more, in varying and uneven amounts. "How can this be?" we queried. She explained that she had made a "faith promise" to the Lord that whatever extra He supplied for her, she would, in turn, give it to the missionaries. She went on exuberantly, "Amazing as it may seem, people started giving me homemade bread and jams and jellies and food from their gardens. I would calculate the value of the gift and send the equivalent money to the mission. For example, someone gave me this new carpet and the carpet layer from church laid it for me for free! Oh, yes, I almost forgot." She then went to her bedroom and brought out an envelope and handed it to me. She continued, "I have been saving for new dentures and this morning I went to the dentist, who examined me and told me I did not need new dentures, that he could make the old ones as good as new, at no charge. So here is the money." Inside the envelope was $200.

During February 2007 I went back to Brazil to help with the construction of an educational facility for native speakers in an interior town located near the headwaters of an Amazon River tributary. A Brazilian mission leader had decided to build an educational center there with the anticipation that several different native language groups would take advantage of the center to study and help the translators with their translation projects.

My friend Ken and I pulled 10,000 feet of wire through flexible conduit and connected the switches, outlets, and light fixtures. Since the boxes were the small metal type, it was difficult to make the connections with "wire nuts"—the typical approved connectors in the U.S. In the electrical store I found small insulated set-screw-type connector pads that would allow me to make the connections within the small boxes. Friday morning I found them and bought ten for $5.00—rather expensive, I thought. That afternoon I realized that I needed ten more so went back to get them. The girl who had waited on me in the morning was not there and the guy who waited on me charged me $5.00—**each**. I knew something was wrong, but there was no way I could prove what the real price was, so I bought them—$50 total. On Saturday I tried to find the same connectors at another store, just to check the price, but could not find them anywhere. All weekend long I was frustrated, feeling that I had been scammed and that I needed to correct the problem. I was losing the spiritual battle and did not enjoy the "victory" God provides.

On Monday morning our team leader told me he was going to the electrical store for some supplies and checked to see if I needed anything. I needed more wire and asked him to get it for me. He no sooner walked in the front door, when the manager saw him, ran up to him, and apologized, "We made a mistake last Friday when we sold your colleague, the tall guy, the connectors and we owe him $45.00." As you know, it wasn't just the returned money that made this "miracle" special, but also my restoration from the spiritual defeat I had suffered under all weekend. God is good!

Harold and Fran were the translators for the M native speakers, a group who lived 500 miles southeast of Brasilia. During that era, Harold and Fran reported that the M people were notorious for fighting, robbing, killing, drunkenness, and strife. They had worked with this group for over twelve years and had even translated some scripture. One or two of the translation helpers had indicated an interest in the Gospel, but a real change and commitment was not apparent. During the Wycliffe conference one year Harold and Fran asked us to pray specifically for a real movement of the Holy Spirit among the M people. After the conference they wanted to return to the M area and visit all the villages to encourage those who had shown interest to make a commitment. However, the four children in their family were all in school and needed someone to stay with them while Harold and Fran were away. Delores and I wanted to help and the teenagers stayed with us while Harold and Fran were gone.

Upon their return Harold and Fran joyously told of visiting three villages and in every village found new believers and a growing and vibrant church. God had answered our prayers and a total of sixty-five people had made the commitment to serve the Lord.

The J language speakers of Brazil displayed a cultural trait that was unique. They had a "taboo" which would not allow repeating of words. If you repeat you somehow are "stealing" the words and causing a curse on them or the speaker. So when Wycliffe translators Bob and Barbara would ask a simple question, like "What do you call this thing I'm sitting on?" the language helper would respond (in his own language) "a chair." But if Bob or Barbara did not quite understand and asked him to repeat his answer, the helper would use different words and say, "A thing to sit on." A third request would result in yet a different answer. This made language learning very difficult and reading impossible, because reading is, in reality, repeating what someone else has said.

All the years we were in Brazil Bob and Barbara were diligently analyzing the language and even tried to get some of the Scriptures translated into J. They were an outstanding example of dedication and persistence. In 1986 when I returned for the national conference of the Brazilian Christian Military I enjoyed the opportunity to visit some of the Wycliffe centers. While I was at Porto Velho over the Mother's Day weekend, Jim, my colleague from Brasília, was also there and arranged for a visit to the J village and asked if I wanted to go along. I was hoping to participate in a worship service in the village since we were going in on a Sunday morning. But when we got off the plane, and asked about a service, we were told there was none as there was only one professing Christian in the village.

We enjoyed fellowshipping and eating Sunday dinner with the missionaries. As we were sitting at the table Bob looked out and saw a woman approaching with two babies, one in each arm, and said, "Here is J history in the making. This is the first time that anyone knows of when the people of the village have let both twins live." (Traditional cultures often do not let both twins live. It may be that there is a spiritual reason, but many say that the mother can not possibly care for two at a time.) I asked why it was that this mother was keeping both twins. "The father is the only Christian in the village," Bob explained. We then went out for a tour of the village. I could feel the heaviness of spiritual darkness as we walked through the village. We came to a straw hut about the size of a large dog house and were told that this was the place that young girls going through puberty were kept for several months. "Is there anyone in there now?" I asked. "No," I was told, "there is a young girl about to go in—but she may not go in." "Why not?" "Because her father is the only Christian in the village."

Fifteen years later Delores and I returned to the J Village—we were in Brazil with our nephew, David McCannell, and we wanted him to experience firsthand the work in a village context. We no sooner got off the plane than we were escorted to the new village chapel. We sat there and enjoyed worship—while the village youth played their guitars and sang their own worship songs. Bob translated for me as I wept for joy! They had no PowerPoint but they had written out the songs on large sheets of paper and would turn the pages to the song they were singing. The twins were there and were very handsome and happy fifteen year-olds. As we walked through the village there was joy and happiness everywhere and I felt no spiritual heaviness at all! And our pilot was collecting notes from the villagers to give to their friends in the city—almost everyone could read and write— with freedom from "taboos".

The details of this amazing transformation are another story, but a few years prior Bob had taken three of his language helpers to a workshop in Porto Velho. During the time there several natives from other tribal villages were baptized. When Bob and his helpers returned to their village, they asked Bob if they also could be baptized. Bob cautiously agreed, "Yes, but we need some training." The next day the three showed up for the training. The following day several more attended. At the end over forty village members completed the training and had accepted Christ as their Savior. They were free! *"...you shall know the truth, and the truth shall make you free."* John 6:32 (New King James Bible)

———

While we were assigned to Dallas in 1978, I was asked by the Director in Brazil to return and help with a special public relations effort, specifically to speak, as part of a Wycliffe team, at a missions conference at a church in São Paulo. I was happy to return to Brazil and enjoyed the conference. I shared some of the stories in this book and was warmly received, especially by the youth. I had to leave a little early, and a group of about twenty young people came with me to the airport and sent me off with hugs and tears. They called me "pastor." I admitted, "I'm just a missionary." They responded, "To us, you're a pastor."

One of the other team members was Helen. She and here partner, Rose, were translators for the K speakers in the Amazon area of Brazil. She told a story that I have often shared since that time. When she was translating the Gospel

of Mark, she employed a young K mother as her translation helper. During the translation effort this young mother
accepted the Lord as her Savior.

After the Gospel of Mark in K was published, the young
mother held it up and asked Helen, "Your mother did not have
this book, did she?" Helen is from Germany and admitted,
"Yes, my mother had this book." "Your grandmother did
not have this book, did she?" "Yes," Helen confessed, "my
grandmother had this book." Then the young mother shared
what was on her heart. "When I was a little girl my grandmother told me that someone was going to come and tell us
how to be free from sin and fear. Why didn't someone come
and tell my grandmother?"

I personally believe that God did call some young man to
go to the K people and share with this grandmother whom He
had prepared to receive the Gospel, but that guy said "No."
Then two generations later, God sent Helen and Rosie to the
K speakers to share the Good News with the granddaughter.
From this experience God again confirmed to me that when
He speaks, it is vitally important to listen and obey!

I must confess that today, as I am writing this in December, it is snowing outside my window here in west-central Minnesota. It is more than snowing—it is the first blizzard of the season. Snow and cold always get me down, and earlier when I was out buying gas and hitching the snow blower up to the tractor I was overwhelmed with discouragement and frustration.

Then I reread some of the stories above and realized that God is still on the throne and has won the victory for us! We can rejoice and be content whatever our situation. My prayer is that these "Sketches of His Presence" will do the same for you.